SCARS OF THE BADGE

SCARS

OF THE

BADGE

FAITH, TRAUMA, AND REDEMPTION

BEHIND THE THIN BLUE LINE

TOM LEE

CROSSBOW
BOLT PRESS

This is a work of nonfiction. The events and experiences described are true to the best of the author's recollection. Some names, details, and identifying characteristics have been changed to protect the privacy of individuals.

The views and opinions expressed in this book are those of the author and do not necessarily reflect the official policy or position of any law enforcement agency, employer, or organization.

First Edition 2026
ISBN (paperback): 979-8-9947204-0-0
ISBN (hardcover): 979-8-9947204-2-4
ISBN (ebook): 979-8-9947204-1-7
Library of Congress Control Number:
2026903144

Published by
Crossbow Bolt Press
Nederland, Texas
www.scarsofthebadge.com

Printed in the United States of America

For my family, immediate and extended alike.

For my wife, who fought beside me long after the uniform came off,
carried the weight of this job with me, and never once walked away.

This book exists because you stayed.

INTRODUCTION

THE SEARING PAIN, LIKE A SUNBURN, ENGULFED MY left arm and the left side of my face: it was not what I imagined it would be. Moments before, I had knocked on the door, and then it happened—the man on the other side kicked the door open. At that moment, I saw him point a crossbow toward me and I ran down the side of the connex trailer that the man lived in. As I drew my weapon to confront the danger this man posed, the pain came.

At that moment, the training and instinct collapsed into something simpler and more dangerous. There was no room for doubt, no space for hesitation, only the belief that decisive, immediate action was the answer. I didn't feel fear so much as focus, a narrowing of the world to threat and response.

In a split second, this moment in time slowed down and thoughts flooded through my head. The only conclusion I could come up with is that I had just been shot. I was already drawing my weapon, and I squeezed a round off from the hip toward the direction of the man with the crossbow. I just wanted him away from me, and the shot I took had done exactly that. Now he was running away, disappearing around the corner of the connex trailer. I had to protect others as well as myself, so I ran to the corner of the trailer to better observe and react to whatever was going to come next.

This wasn't the first time I had been in danger; I was seventeen years into my law enforcement career by this time and had seen many ups and downs. I had been fired from my first agency, worked as a wrecker driver, seen redemption, and began a new start. How did I get to the point of being shot in the face with a crossbow?

CHAPTER ONE

COLLEGE

TO ANSWER THE ABOVEMENTIONED QUESTION, I HAVE to go back to the summer of 2001. I graduated from Garland Christian Academy. I was an average student, but did not follow my high school's recommendation to go to a Christian college, as I was bored with school. I knew where I wanted to be for my career—computer-controlled heating and air conditioning—and a Christian college was just going to put that goal further out of reach instead of accelerate it. I had already been accepted into a university with a prestigious engineering program within driving distance from my parents' home, so I would not have to worry about campus housing. I was proud that I was able to go to this university. In the early 2000s, the sense was that if you wanted to succeed in life, you needed to get a college degree. Almost everyone I knew was headed to college or the military.

I had worked for my dad's air conditioning and heating company since I could remember. My dad had started his business on the side after working for the maintenance department of a school district.

It's Texas, and it's HOT in the summer, so everyone needs the cool air from the air conditioning, and those things break all the time. It did not take long for my dad's business to grow, and I found myself tagging along with him every chance I could.

During the summer breaks from school, I did not want to be out playing like all the other kids; I wanted to be working with my dad. Although I was only a teenager, because I was already working and even though it was for my dad, I felt as though I was an adult. I loved the electrical part of the job: relays, switches, thermostats, and other components all working together to make the systems operate, which I found all fascinating. So of course I wanted to go to college and work in the same field; the thought of policing never entered my mind then.

I was starting college, and as part of the new student orientations, student groups lined the hallways of the gym. These organizations attempt to draw you in and get you to join their group, consisting of engineering societies, the fraternities and sororities, and many more. If you are interested in a subject, there is probably a student organization out there that's also interested in the same thing. They are all vying for attention and support of the students. It just so happened that the university Police Department also had a table setup, and they were promoting a student organization that allows students to learn about law enforcement, The university Police Explorers program. Why did this group draw my eye? Was it because one of my dad's friends was a police officer? Was it because I had some interactions with the police officers who went to the church I grew up in, and I had always looked up to these guys?

Was it because during my senior year in high school, I was at my friend's house, and we were outside talking in the backyard when I heard a commotion in the front yard and went out there to investigate? When I opened the gate from the backyard, there was someone inside my vehicle stealing the radio, amp, and speakers. Anger swelled in me as I saw the man taking my stuff. What do you do as a high school student when you catch someone stealing from you? Well, I'm still not sure, but I can tell you what I did.

I slammed the door on the guy and locked him in my vehicle as my friend ran to get her parents. I thought closing him in my vehicle would contain him, and then the police would get there and arrest him. However, the guy ended up kicking open the vehicle door and started to run. *What do I do now?* I thought. *If he gets away, he won't be held responsible for what he has done.* Thankfully, I was able to catch up and tackle him. The guy laid on his back with his hands up as I stood over him until the police showed up. The next day, I found his wallet in my vehicle and took it to the police station to turn in. There was such an adrenaline rush from capturing this guy, and of course, everyone got to hear me tell the tale the next week at school.

Also during my senior year of high school, the same friend had her vehicle stolen from her house. She called me upset about her car being stolen, and I headed over to her house to talk to her about what she knew. While driving to her house, I looked down every road I passed, keeping an eye out for her vehicle. Soon, I found her stolen vehicle, wrecked on a side street a couple miles from her house. The police officer that came and took the report when I found the vehicle did not treat my friend well and accused her of wrecking the vehicle and reporting it stolen so she would not get in trouble with her parents. This made her cry, which made me mad and wonder how someone could be so cold and callous to someone who had just lost a piece of her identity to a thief.

I really don't know what the attraction was, but there I was at the Police Explorer table, asking questions about the organization and how to get involved while pursuing my life's dream of working on HVAC electrical systems. I found myself in my first semester of college taking chemistry, pre-calculus, Texas history; you know, all the exciting stuff. I also started attending the Explorer meetings and was actually excited to meet the campus police officers, do ride-alongs with them, and get a basic understanding of the job of a police officer.

CHAPTER TWO

9/11

ON THE MORNING OF SEPTEMBER 11, 2001, I FOUND MY-self as a college freshman with an 8 a.m. chemistry lab. We were doing whatever chemistry experiments we were assigned to do that day, but everything seemed so quiet, almost eerie. I can tell you that an 8 a.m. chemistry lab isn't one that a lot of students sign up for.

Before class, I did hear on the radio that a plane had crashed into the World Trade Center, but at that time, the second aircraft had not hit the other building yet, and so we didn't really have a grasp on what was really going on. The TA came into the room and said that a second plane had just hit the World Trade Center. It was dead silent after that news; everyone knew it was no accident. I wanted to find out who did this and seek justice for innocent lives. So, I hurried to finish my labwork and then headed to the Student Union, where there was a giant TV. The room was packed; I did not know it at the time, but this was going to be a pivotal point in my life. No longer was I going to be dreaming of electrical systems; I now wanted to find a way to rid the world of this evil, but it would take me a year to figure this new approach out.

The semester ended, and I enrolled in the standard classes to continue my electrical engineering degree. I also took the U.S. and Texas Government class the next semester where I found myself highly engaged and enjoying the government class, but lacking interest and falling behind in the other classes for this degree. I was yearning for something deeper, something where I could make a difference in this world. The events of 9/11 had shown me that evil was lurking around every corner.

What I didn't recognize then was how comforting that belief was. Seeing the world in terms of good and evil made everything feel clearer, more ordered, as if the lines were finally drawn where they belonged. If evil existed, then confronting it gave me purpose to action and direction to ambition. It narrowed my focus in a way that felt righteous and necessary at the time, even as it quietly left less room for doubt, nuance, or grace.

While on summer break, the university Police Department developed the idea to allow the Explorers to fill in for the dispatchers, so they sent a couple of us to the Texas DPS TCIC/NCIC class: TCIC/NCIC is the Texas Crime Information Center and the National Crime Information Center, a database that connects law enforcement agencies around the world but mostly just in the United States. The system is what gives driver's license, vehicle license plate, and warrant information. This was the answer I was looking for—with more income. Working for my dad was great, but there was only enough work in the summer. This opportunity provided a more stable income, yet no benefits (paid time off, medical insurance, etc.) because it was a student worker position.

In August of 2002, I officially started as a dispatcher with the university Police Department. I talked with one of the officers and told him I was thinking about changing my career; he encouraged me to make the move. So I started taking criminal justice classes at the local community college instead of going to the university for classes. Some of my best friends and ones I still speak to today come from this period of my life.

CHAPTER THREE

FIRST POLICE ACADEMY

IN 2003, THE UNIVERSITY HIRED ME AS A DISPATCHER, giving me a full-time job in police work, paid time off, and the benefits of insurance and retirement. I got placed on the evening shift, which was 3 p.m. to 11 p.m.; that was by far the most active shift. I was having a blast with my new job: this entailed making traffic stops, breaking up alcohol-fueled parties, and catching drug dealers. The officers were working together as one, identifying drug dealers, working their way into their circles, and then executing search and arrest warrants. Being on this shift was satisfying, but I longed for something more. I needed to be in the heat of the moment, not just on the sidelines assisting. It was not long before I decided to put myself through a police academy part time while continuing to dispatch for the university. Thankfully, the training I had already received from the Explorer program made the academics of the police academy a breeze. I never studied for any of the tests, but I was always one of the first ones to finish. I did not even have to study to take the State Police Exam to get my license.

There I was; twenty-two and certified to be a police officer in Texas. Now I just had to find an agency to hire me. There are so many agencies to consider in a state the size of Texas. Although the Texas State Troopers were always a draw because of their statewide police authority and opportunities for advancement, the drawback was that you could be assigned anywhere in the state. The big city police departments mostly make you go through their police academies and having already put myself through one academy, I did not want to go through another to join their force.

Getting hired by a police department is hard, as they require everyone to complete a fifty-plus-page personal history statement, where they ask you everything about your life, your families' lives, your bank account information, your alcohol and drug use history, and more. You have to fill a different personal history statement out to every agency you apply to, along with the standard hiring application. Unfortunately, I had been passed over by every department I had applied at, being told: "You're too young; you need more life experience." The rejection, and that statement, were crushing.

Some time later, the university Police Department where I worked finally had an opening. I started their process, and it felt like the whole agency was rooting me on. I have never been a long-distance runner, and being on the bigger side of the scale, the mile and a half run in under 15 minutes and 50 seconds for consideration was always an issue for me. The pushups and situps were not problems but that run … every night when I got off work, I would come home from dispatching and would run the block a few times around my parents' house. On test day, everyone on duty came out to cheer us on; it's a small department, so you know everyone. I had made it to the last quarter mile but I was fading fast. It was hard to breathe, and my lungs and legs were burning. I just needed it to be over already.

At the time, I didn't understand what I was teaching myself. Pushing through the pain, ignoring doubt, and refusing to stop felt like proof that I belonged. Endurance became its own kind of validation, a belief that if I could just outlast the discomfort, I would earn my place and silence any question about whether I was enough or not. It was a lesson that served me well in the academy, even as it quietly trained me to ignore warning signs of what was ahead, signs that I wouldn't recognize until much later.

One of the on-duty officers, who was a friend named Kendra, came out there and started running with me to make sure I finished on time. Thankfully, I passed that run in plenty of time to be in the same department I was in for dispatching and as an Explorer. The university Police Department was its own autonomous police department, but the university system had a system police department that oversaw all the individual police departments. The thing about the university Police Department is I would have to go back through their system police academy, which was in Austin, Texas, even though I had already passed an academy and was licensed by the state. I thought the hardest part was behind me; in reality, the real tests were only beginning.

CHAPTER FOUR

UNIVERSITY POLICE ACADEMY

THE UNIVERSITY POLICE ACADEMY WAS LOCATED WEST of Austin on an old missile base in the Texas Hill Country. Everyone at the academy was already hired by one of the university components. Most of us were from other areas of Texas; therefore, the university Academy put us all up in hotels for six months and provided us a per diem check for six months of food. Being in my early twenties, this was the largest amount of money I had ever had. I got a check for doing my job (attending the academy), and they also paid for all my living expenses. Not to mention the pay for being a police officer was $37,000, more than the $24,000 I was making as a dispatcher. I was eager to start the academy so I could move into my new passion of policing, as it felt like I was already in the place I needed to be. However, I was about to find out that this academy was going to test me more than I knew.

Now the classes were mostly the same from the first academy, but each academy had different strengths and weaknesses. The university Academy was very robust and was several hundred hours longer than the previous academy I attended. Most of the university Police Academy was academic, but they had a PT program as well where we were required to do drills every Monday, Wednesday, and Friday. Their facility did not have showers or lockers so PT was always done in the afternoon, in Texas, in the summer. With the heat, I would finish each PT session worn out and drenched in sweat. PT normally consisted of a mile and a half or longer run, push-up, sit-ups, and various other strength and stretching exercises to show your abilities.

I have already told you I am not the best runner out there, and now they were throwing in the hills and heat, which made the process less than desirable for me. The first week of the academy, we had to do the run all over again. It was hot that day when we did the run. When I started running, in no time, it felt like my feet were concrete, making every step just that much harder. I did not make the run time needed and was so disappointed in myself, feeling like I had let down myself as well as all the people who had been cheering me on. It was not the end though; I would keep pushing on throughout my time at the academy.

At the end of the academy, we were supposed to complete the one-and-a-half-mile run about a minute faster than when we entered the academy. However, it was now November, and things were much different. It was a cold windy day for the run, and the air itself stung when you breathed in and took your breath away. I felt good about the run and was on a good pace, one that would bring me near the time needed to complete the run on time, even at about a minute faster than the previous run. The last quarter mile is where I was going to finish strong so I picked up the pace and sprinted to the end. The instructor called out the time as soon as I crossed the finish line: 14:54. I missed the needed time by four seconds.

It crushed me to not pass that requirement on the first attempt. I wondered what my department thought about the failure and was scared I was about to get kicked out of the academy, ultimately losing my chance at being a police officer. Thankfully, the academy allowed me and another cadet to do the run again. The instructors also allowed someone to run with you and encourage you along the way. When I started losing my pace during the run, they would gently put their hand on my back and push me forward. They also had us run the second time on a course that had some downhill slopes but was still one and a half miles long. I passed the second attempt about two minutes faster than the entrance time that was required and was so thankful.

The university Academy also brought in specialized groups to train us. Austin's Bomb Squad taught us about explosives: det cord, blasting caps, plastic explosives. We were given a basic overview and also witnessed a watermelon being blown up for us. The Travis County Constable's office did a presentation on mental health. A Texas DPS trooper did two weeks of physical confrontations and fighting techniques. The fighting was tough, and the trooper would have you go run a half-mile with an obstacle course. As soon as you got back to the gym, you immediately laid on your back, and the trooper or another instructor would get on top of you and start choking you. You had to fight your way out of the choke hold for several minutes.

We also did training with pepper spray, otherwise known as OC spray, and CS gas, otherwise known as tear gas. Those sessions required you to be exposed to the substance in preparation for real-life situations. Our tear gas exposure was not nearly as bad as the military does it, as they just made us walk through the chemical as it was being released.

What mattered more than the severity of the exposure was what it normalized. Being forced to function through pain, confusion, and physical distress was framed as preparation for being a police officer. As proof that discomfort could be managed and overridden, each exercise reinforced that same quiet lesson: the body reacts, but the job demands control. At the time, that felt like strength. I didn't yet realize how easily that mindset could slip from resilience to numbness.

Pepper spray, on the other hand, was rough. They had us all line up, and when it was your turn, you stood in front of an instructor and closed your eyes. Your signal to the instructor that you were ready, was to open your eyes. As soon as he saw your eyes start to open, he blasted you right in the face with it. It got on everything and burned. The burning was different for everyone, but it took me about forty-five minutes to recover from being sprayed with pepper spray. One of the worst things about pepper spray is long after it is over, when you shower that night, it reactivates, and you get it again, the burning sensation.

During the defensive tactics portion of the academy, they had one drill where they placed us in a circle and had one cadet get in the center of the circle. People from the group would then randomly run at the person in the center, simulating getting attacked from all directions and not knowing where it came from. When I was in the center, one female who was in the class ran to my back side. I was barely able to get turned around to try and deflect her away from me. She went flying instead and landed on her wrist, which broke. I was just trying to defend myself from her attack and deflect her away from me. The other cadets blamed me for her broken wrist, saying I pushed her like I did because I did not want women in policing. Where was this belief coming from? There were four women in my class of eighteen, and I never had a problem with any of them. Their assumption was absolutely false, but then again, they did not know that a female police officer, Kendra, had pushed me to where I was. I resented being labeled something that was not in the slightest bit true. My chief and assistant chief were females. Anger swelled in me at this accusation, but I could not allow anyone else to see that. I just had to brush it off and continue to prove myself.

Although the academics were tough, having previously completed the state test allowed me to breeze through that part of the academy. At the end of the academy, all the cadets got together and went out to celebrate passing the academy. The next day, all our families were going to be there to watch our swearing-in ceremony. Once we were sworn in, we were officially police officers, with all the authority that went with it.

At the swearing-in ceremony, my mom and sister were in attendance, but my father decided to stay home because of his health issues, having been diagnosed with chronic obstructed pulmonary disease. Throughout the academy, I had called my dad nearly every night to update him on the things we were doing at the academy. I had hoped he was able to make it, but I understood he did not feel up to it. When the ceremony was over, the state trooper who taught our academy spotted me and told me good job finishing the academy, and that if I ever needed anything, I knew where to find him. I felt like I was being considered a coworker now and not just a cadet.

I had a couple days off after the ceremony, and then it was time to begin a new chapter in my life that I was eager to start.

CHAPTER FIVE

FIRST DAYS AS A POLICE OFFICER

IN DECEMBER 2005, I GRADUATED FROM THE UNIVERSIty Police Academy and was commissioned as a police officer for the university. I was given a couple days off to move everything back to Dallas and then was assigned to show up on night shift to begin my field training; it just so happened that Kendra was assigned as my first phase FTO (field training officer). Field training is where you are paired with a training officer and throughout the process, you do more and more of the tasks of the officer. The final phase is a ghost phase where the training officer just observes you.

I was given all the essentials to be an officer for my uniform: five short-sleeve shirts, three long-sleeve shirts, five pairs of pants; an outer belt consisting of a pepper spray, gun and holster, magazines, magazine holder, an extendable baton, radio, flashlight ring, and two sets of handcuffs with cases. They also gave me a ballistic vest to wear under my uniform shirt, as well as a winter jacket and a rain jacket. The only thing that was not provided was underwear and black polishable boots.

On my first day as a police officer, when I showed up, the evening shift had made a drug arrest, and they wanted me to transport the person to jail. When someone is booked into jail on a drug charge, the jail requires a strip search. My FTO was a female, and the person arrested was a male; that meant it was all on me to do the strip search. I knew this was a part of the job, but I just did not know it was going to be the first part as a newly sworn-in officer. I thought to myself: *Okay, let's just get this over with, and hopefully he does not have anything else hidden.* A strip search is having someone go into a secluded restroom, strip to nakedness, bend over while holding their buttocks open, and coughing to make sure they have not hidden anything in their rectum. I put on some throw-away nitrile gloves because no one wants to touch anything that came out of someone else.

The gloves were practical, but they were also symbolic in ways I didn't recognize. They created a barrier, a barrier between not only me and whatever I would be handling, but also the person it came from. Distance makes it easier, allowing me to focus on the task without absorbing the human weight attached to it. That separation felt necessary, even professional, and I didn't yet understand how often the job would ask me to choose distance as a form of self-preservation.

I can still hear the snap of the cold, tight-fitting gloves and the sight of the light tan walls of that restroom. I couldn't believe that this was my first act as a police officer. There was no subtle entrance; it was a big wham, here you go. So the first hour of working as a police officer, here I was looking at another guy's butt, making sure he did not have any contraband up there. What an introduction to policing that was.

There were times during that first month that I hated the field training program. It did not help that my training officer, Kendra, was always worried about everything in general. There was one night very early in the morning when we saw a vehicle she just knew was speeding. We did not use radar to check its speed, but she had me stop it for speeding. I did not understand how the stop would be lawful without radar, but she was my training officer, and I had to do what she told me to do. Later, I understood the principle of reasonable suspicion versus probable cause, but at this instant, I was at a loss.

I approached the vehicle and made contact with the sole occupant in the vehicle. They gave me their out-of-state driver's license and told me they were a contractor working on one of the new buildings on campus. I went back to the patrol vehicle and had the dispatcher run his license through the computer system. Every time you hear the dispatcher call your number and ask if you are clear to copy, your heart jumps a little bit. They are about to give you some information they don't want the suspect to know that you know. It could be warrants, it could be a known offense, but there's always a tense moment before you get the information that they want to give you. I waited while watching the sky start lightening up and the sun creeping toward the horizon to start the new day.

Dispatch came back on the radio and said the man was wanted for an out-of-state felony probation violation. Hearing this can make you uneasy; there was no way the suspect didn't know that he had violated his probation. Was he going to run? Was he going to fight? Was he going to comply? Those were decisions he was going to have to make. That started one of those high-risk vehicle stops we talked about earlier. Every officer is supposed to point their gun at the violator in case he decides he wants to fight while you are ordering him out of the vehicle.

I drew my gun to begin the felony stop; that's when Kendra told me I needed to keep my gun holstered because she was worried something bad might happen. It was pretty absurd to me that she thought I might accidentally shoot this man if I did not have a reason to shoot him or that I could not use the PA at the same time.

That's demoralizing as an officer. I hadn't earned her trust yet so I did as she asked, but I knew the exact words I was going to say on the PA to get him out of the vehicle in the safest manner possible. How much more do I have to do to "make it"? All I had to do was work the PA system and give the orders to the guy. If something bad did happen, I was going to have to take valuable seconds to pull my gun and engage the suspect, thinking about the safety of everyone during this time. I do not remember now why the PA system was possibly not working properly in our vehicle, but another officer ended up giving the orders over their PA system, and I made sure to draw my gun now and was not going to look at Kendra for approval. I just did what I knew needed to be done. Nothing bad happened, and the suspect was arrested without trouble.

The next month, I was rotated to day shift for the second of four phases of field training, and it was then that my life changed in an instant. It was during the first week of being on day shift, on one of my off days, and I was planning on sleeping in a bit. My mom woke me early that morning in a panic, and I did not know what was going on. The second time she called for me, I realized it was something important.

There was a heaviness I could not explain. Nothing had been said yet, but my body reacted before my mind could catch up. A sudden clarity that whatever waited for me in the other room would not be routine. I had already learned to read tension on traffic stops and dispatch calls; that same instincts surfaced here, uninvited. Something was wrong, and no amount of training or preparation was going to change what I was about to see.

I jumped up and ran to the living room; that's when I saw my dad lying on the couch. His leg had a dark redness where it hung off the couch. I touched his wrist to check for a pulse and immediately felt his cold skin between my fingers. There was no doubt that my father had died in his sleep. I called 911 and told them my father had died, and that they needed to send the police to document the incident. The police soon arrived, as with all deaths, and started an investigation. When they went to remove my father's body, the officer attempted to get us all to go to a back room while this was happening, but I was having none of that. I was going to watch everything that happened, being pretty numb to the whole thing at this point. I needed some alone time, some time all to myself where I could grieve.

Being alone felt safer than being witnessed. Grief didn't fit anywhere where I knew how to carry it, as I had already learned how to function, how to stay composed, how to keep moving when things went wrong. Sitting with the weight of what had happened to my dad felt less like healing and more like exposure. I choose to isolate myself instead, believing that control and quiet were the same as strength.

Like a good police officer, I maintained my stoic persona and did not allow it to faze me, at least so I thought. The only time I cried was when I was alone in my truck. I was hurting inside, but I was going to be a rock on the outside. I had to be a rock, because I did not know who I was without control. The job had taught me that composure was currency, that calm meant competent, and competent meant belonging. If I showed cracks, I worried they would be read as weakness, not grief. I believed that holding myself together was how I would honor my father. How I stayed functional. How I proved I could still be trusted with responsibility. Letting myself fall apart felt like indulgent, even dangerous, so I chose steadiness instead, unaware of how much effort it was costing me to maintain it.

At the funeral viewing for my father, only Terry McCurry showed up from my department, the person who was going to be my third-phase field training officer. I will never forget that he took the time out of his day to show up to my father's viewing. He might not have been the only person from the department who came to the funeral, but I don't remember anyone else being there but him. It really was a big blur for me, and so many people were hugging me and shaking my hand after the funeral, I just cannot remember anyone who was there. I still felt lost without my dad as he was my rock and someone who had always been there for me no matter what.

I didn't fully understand how much of my idea of strength came from watching him. My father showed up. He worked. He endured. He didn't complain, and he didn't ask for much in return. In losing him, I wasn't just grieving the man. I was losing the model I had followed my entire life. Without realizing it, I tried to replace his steadiness with my own, believing that being dependable meant being unshakable; it felt like that was the only way I knew how to move forward.

The department made me take a week off of work, though I wanted to continue to prove myself and wanted to go back to work. In retrospect, that was probably a wise decision on their part. The next week, I was back to work. It was a weekend day, either a Saturday or Sunday, and it was early morning. I was driving as my second-phase FTO, Raymond, was in the passenger seat. He looked over at me and asked if stop signs apply to police officers. I told him they did unless you were in an emergency or otherwise had a good reason to run the stop sign. That's when he asked me if that's true, why didn't I stop for the last stop sign? What just happened? I did not realize I had not stopped for the stop sign and was so embarrassed that I had run the stop sign. Inside, I was trying to pick up the pieces in my mind and make a picture of the situation that occurred, but I did not realize that my head was not in the game at work.

When I was in the third phase of FTO, Terry took up for me, especially during an incident where I was wrongfully accused. There was a disturbance call where the administration went back and watched the video. The camera was to my back, and my right hand was resting on my mag pouches in the front of my duty belt. The administration was trying to say my hand was in my pocket. The problem with their assessment was: (1) my gun was blocking the pocket, and (2) I have large legs, and the administration did not have us fitted for the uniforms. They just ordered stuff off the internet, so the pants were really tight around my thighs, making it very uncomfortable to have my hands in my pocket or really anything in the pockets. Terry told the administration they were wrong, and I did not have my hands in my pocket.

Some of you are probably wondering why it's a big deal whether my hands were in my pockets or not and I get it, but it all has to do with being ready for whatever may come in any kind of situation. If your hands are in your pockets and if someone all of a sudden attacks you, it takes you that much longer to get your hands out of your pocket and defend yourself. By not putting your hands in your pockets, you save valuable time to protect yourself during an attack.

What bothered me more than the discomfort was how easily context disappeared once a judgment was made. The explanation did not matter, only how it looked on camera. I learned that day that perception could outweigh reality and that defending yourself often came second to accepting the narrative already forming among other people. It reinforced a lesson I was still trying to absorb. Stay composed, don't argue, and keep moving forward. Questioning the interpretation felt riskier than enduring the misunderstanding.

I can't separate that moment from where I was mentally at the time this all happened. My father's death hadn't made me careless, but it had split my attention in ways I didn't yet recognize. I was present, but not fully settled. Capable, but still carrying weight I did not know how to set down. That experience showed me how quickly performance can be judged without context, and how little space there is in policing for grief to exist alongside competence. I never heard again about having my hands in my pockets.

Finally, after three and a half months, I had proven myself to all my FTOs, and now it was my turn to prove it to myself that I was ready to be an officer.

CHAPTER SIX

POLICE OFFICER

THERE'S SOMETHING ABOUT THE FIRST DAY YOU ARE released from field training, and now you are doing it all on your own. There is so much power and responsibility that you are given in this job, where there is no one in the passenger seat to help if something goes wrong. There is no one to tell you that you should do something this way or that way.

Freedom is intoxicating, but it comes with a cost I hadn't fully considered. There was no buffer, no one to share the responsibility if something went wrong. I had been trained how to act decisively and confidently, and now there was nothing to soften the consequences of those instincts when part of real-world situations.

That first day is exciting and terrifying all at the same time. I was in control, and I got to steer the direction of how my day was going to shape up. At this point, I could do a traffic stop, answering a call for a disturbance, or anything else. The first traffic stop I had to do solo, I was nervous heading into it but as soon as it started, the procedures flowed like I had been doing them for years. Maybe I did know what I was doing. Anytime anything goes wrong, you are the first person on scene and the one everyone is looking at for answers. I was twenty-four years old at that time, and everyone expected me to have all the answers as a police officer, or at least that's how it felt. Now it was time for me to figure out my policing style and what I was good at.

After that first day, that feeling of excitement and nerves never comes back or at least never feels like it felt that day. You start learning things and expanding what you are comfortable doing. Soon, I found my niche area doing something most cops do not want to do but there is an abundance of them on college campuses: driving while intoxicated (DWI) cases. I had worked at the police department for three years as a dispatcher, and I had not seen any of the officers do a DWI stop yet, so I wanted to be the first.

The memory of the first DWI stop I made is fairly vivid, even though it was twenty years ago. I learned so much from that stop, though I was so nervous about everything. I was running all the tests through my head over and over again to make sure I did not miss a step. I talked to the driver, after I pulled him over, and he said the thing that I would learn most drunks say: "I only had two drinks." I smelled the odor I would become all too familiar with during these stops. The odor of sweat mixed with a stale sweet hue that denotes an alcoholic beverage.

The smell became a marker for me. Before the tests were complete or the paperwork was started, it told a story that the driver was not going to be able to talk his way out of. I learned to trust those early signals. Even though everything was new, I was learning how to read people, how to separate nerves from instinct, and how to trust my own observations without letting fear take over.

When I got the driver out of the car, he was able to walk to the back of the car, but he was stumbling over his feet. My voice was shaky as I gave him the verbatim instructions for the field sobriety tests. I hoped the suspect and the camera didn't pick up on me being as nervous as the suspect, as one missed step and an attorney could get the whole thing thrown out of court.

I checked off every step in my head, and as the suspect followed my pen with his eyes, I could see his pupil jerking back and forth. On the one leg stand test, he swayed back and forth. He even hopped to try to keep from putting his foot down. It was obvious he was intoxicated, so he was arrested and taken to jail. Thankfully, I made it through this first stop and set my sights on being great at future stops.

Unfortunately, they tell you horror stories in the academy about doing DWI stops. These stops also generate a mountain of paperwork. Most of that paperwork is a check box and filling in the blank documents, which makes them super easy in reality, but everyone tends to get so caught up in it that they hate doing them. It got to the point that I was doing two or three DWIs a week, but I loved it. Rarely was there a weekend night I worked that someone did not go to jail for DWI. There are so many stories about how many people's lives have been forever changed because of a DWI accident (which I will share later in the book).

I have already mentioned that some of my best friends came from this period of time, and they started finding police jobs with agencies around the area. One of the lieutenants who worked at the university Police Department left to be a chief of police for a small town on the border of Collin, Grayson, and Fannin County in Texas. Several of my friends either went to work for him or began serving as a reserve officer, a part-time, unpaid law enforcement officer who worked shifts alongside full-time officers.

Those relationships mattered more than I realized at the time. Working alongside people who were willing to show up without pay, without recognition, just to do the job shaped how I viewed law enforcement and my place in it. It was not just about the badge or the hours worked. It was the shared nights, shared exhaustion, and knowing the person next to you was there because they wanted to be. That sense of camaraderie carried into everything we did, especially on nights when the calls slowed and the job felt less like survival and more like routine.

Now the night shift got a little slow at four in the morning, so we ended up calling each other about this time of the morning because we knew we were at work, but things would probably be slow. We would meet up for breakfast when we got off work before heading home to sleep; there's nothing like steak and eggs right before you go to sleep. Food always seems to build strong relationships.

Those meals were a relief valve. A place where the weight of the night could be set down, even if it was just for a little while. We didn't always talk about what was bothering us directly, but the conversations mattered just the same. Being around people who understood the job, without the explanation or pretense, made the long nights easier and the hard calls bearable.

Just like most friends do, we would talk about work and even try to one up each other with the stories from the night. Sometimes they had the better story and sometimes I would have the better story. My stories normally had the same theme, so I stopped this drunk driver and blah blah blah happened. One of the other guys always had a taser story.

Most of the people who left the university Police Department did not leave on the best terms, as things at the department were on a slow spiral downward. The administration and the boots on the ground guys were not on the same page. So I would go visit with them at their departments on my days off and ride out with them. They were not allowed to do the same because of their histories with the university Police Department. Through whatever means, the department heard rumors that I was riding out with these other departments and told me that it was unwise for me to ride out with my friends, but I continued anyway. Being told not to do it didn't feel like guidance; it felt like an overreach into a part of my life I still believed belonged to me.

The second or third time I rode with my friends, I was getting comfortable with being the rebel. One day, it was near the end of shift, and it had been a long slow day in the world of policing. We pulled into the station, and I decided to go home while my friend finished up the end-of-shift paperwork. I started driving out of the city down the tiny highway and had gotten approximately a mile away from the police department in an area where one portion of this road dipped down and had a bridge over it.

When I made it closer to the bridge, I noticed something was hanging from it. The closer I got, the thing hanging from the bridge came into better focus. It was not something hanging from the bridge, but rather someone was hanging from it. My heart felt like it leapt out of my chest. It had been sometime, at least a couple hours, since we had driven this part of the road so I did not have a clue how long the person had been there. There were walls on both sides of the road, and I really did not know the layout of the city or how to get on top of the bridge. I needed help from my on-duty friend.

I drove back to the police station and alerted my friend, and we both jumped in the patrol car and started driving back to the scene. He knew where he was going and drove to the top of the bridge. The whole time, things were flashing through my head about having to write a report at my police department about the incident and how was the chief going to take it all. With them telling me it was unwise to go do ride-outs with people who had left the department on not the best terms, I didn't think the chief was going to like me having to do a report about it. Not to mention the fact I was going to have to deal with this death. My friend looked over the bridge and saw the body with a rope there at the top of the bridge. He began to pull on the rope and pull the person up.

While watching him, it didn't seem like he was having any issues pulling the person up. That seemed odd, and then all of a sudden, the body came over the side of the bridge. It wasn't a person; it was a scarecrow. There was straw coming out of the top of the shirt, and it did not have hands or feet. Someone had hung a scarecrow off the bridge, much to my relief. To this day, I have lingering questions about whether my friend had any involvement with this. Obviously, someone was pranking us, or was it just a prank on me? It wasn't about tricking anyone or crossing the line; it was just dumb humor.

Speaking of pranks, we were notorious for pranking each other and other people, as we derived pleasure from pranks we pulled on each other. Cops in general have a tendency to do pranks on other cops. From ill-smelling things being left under the seats, pepper spray being applied to door handles, or rocks placed in the hub caps of vehicles, which make an awful sound when you drive. I even once took some painter's tape to a state trooper's car. The vehicle was black, and the letters were white. So, with blue painter's tape, I hurriedly used a marker to color it black. I strategically placed pieces of tape on the white letters of the black car.

It was a moment of levity in a job that rarely allowed it. A reminder that before the calls, the reports, and the consequences, we are still human. The now-black tape blotted out parts of the white letters and the trooper's vehicle read ATE POOP instead of STATE TROOPER on the rear of the vehicle and STATE POOPER on the right side of the vehicle. I was not able to make it to the driver's side when he came out of the jail, which made things better. He did not notice the changes to his vehicle and left the jail with the changes on his car. I snapped a few photos with my cell phone and immediately sent it to all my friends. It's not every day you see a STATE POOPER on the roadway. I know it's juvenile, but sometimes making people laugh is the best medicine. What do you expect out of young guys in their twenties who are bored in the middle of the night with little to no supervision? I was learning that not only do you need medicine to heal you physically, but you also need medicine in the form of laughter to heal your mind, especially in law enforcement.

Humor didn't last, even in funny moments like that. I was on patrol one night, driving around campus through all the parking lots, doing all the normal mundane things police do. It was approaching the witching hour when all the DWIs would be out and about. At this time, I had become proficient with DWIs and looked for them as often as I could. I had the radar going, the dispatch radio on, and was listening to music. There were hardly any cars on the road as I drove the streets. Suddenly, my radar started showing someone coming toward me doing 58 mph in a 45-mph zone.

I was paying attention to the lanes to the left of me (oncoming lanes) while ascending a hill. I was scouring the lanes, looking for the vehicle that was speeding, but wasn't finding one that looked like it was doing the speed the radar had stated. The radar was continuously showing a vehicle was going 58 mph. As I crested the hill, I caught some light straight ahead of me and had just enough time to slam on the brakes and yank the steering wheel to the right, barely missed having a head-on collision with the vehicle.

I made a U-turn in the middle of the street and turned on my emergency lights. Both of us were now traveling the wrong way down the road. That's a strange feeling the first time you do it. You may not know this, but there are several indicators to tell you you're on the wrong side of the road. The most shocking one to me was all the reflectors on the roadways, the ones between the line stripes that normally reflect white. Well when you drive the wrong way down the road, they are no longer white but red.

The vehicle stopped and pulled over to the right like you are supposed to do when getting stopped by the police. There was just one problem with this—pulling to the right placed us in the left lane of the flow of traffic. I had to worry about cars coming toward us, and I did not have any of the flashing emergency lights on my vehicle to alert other drivers we were stopped there. It did not take long before another officer showed up and parked on the other side of the street, protecting us from traffic.

Now traditionally you don't put the suspect between you because if he decides to do something stupid, you don't want to be in a crossfire situation, but what do you do in this instance? We chose the adapt-and-overcome method of the crossfire possibility being better for us than getting hit by a car that did not realize we were there. Once the officer walked over to me, I had him watch the guy for a minute or so because I needed time to regroup myself after almost getting hit. My life had just flashed before my eyes. I was not just working and playing a cat-and-mouse game. There was much more at stake here, and I could have easily been dealing with a lifelong injury or death. A couple minutes later, I continued the stop, doing all the field sobriety tests on the driver and determining he was intoxicated. I then took him to jail for DWI. This was my first brush with death, but it wouldn't be my last.

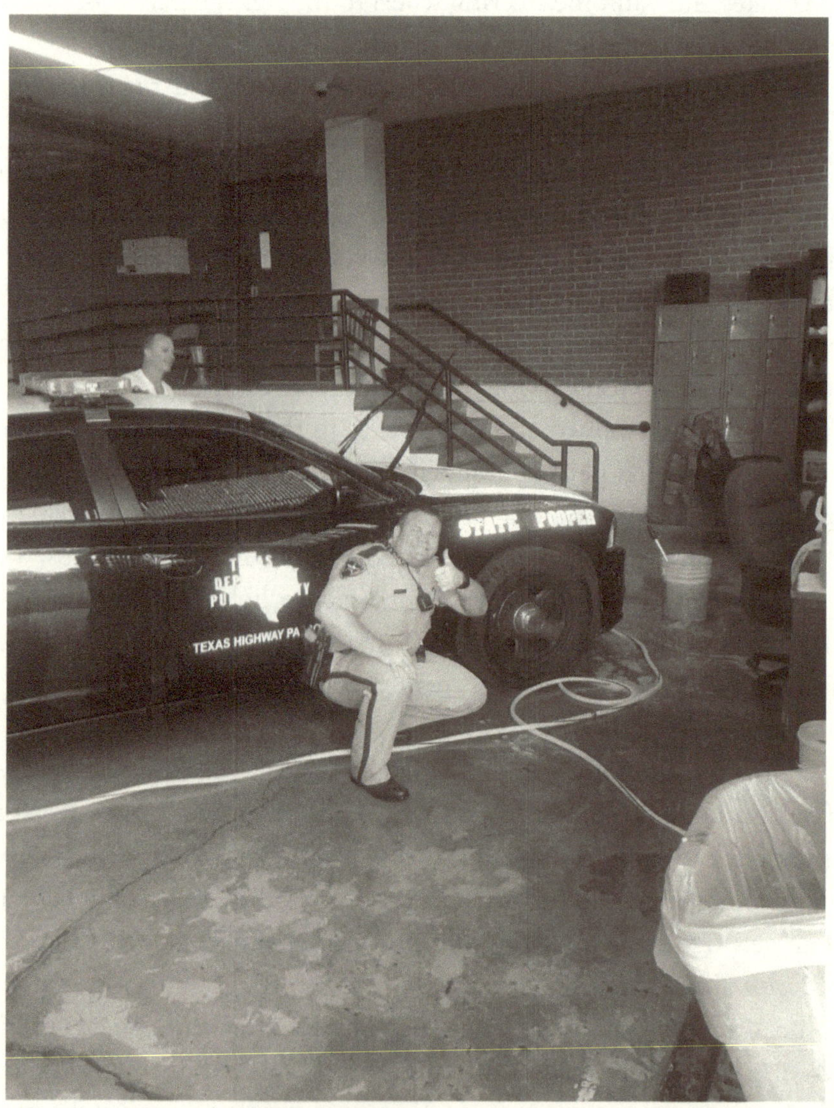

CHAPTER FIVE

FIRST PURSUIT

ONE NIGHT, I WAS OUT LOOKING FOR DWIS AND MADE a traffic stop on a car, which turned down the next road and stopped. I exited my vehicle and approached the car. When I got to about the trunk of the car, the driver floored the gas pedal.

I ran back to my patrol vehicle. My adrenaline was pumping, my heart was racing. About the time I was able to put my car in drive and begin chasing the car, the car turned left and ran over the center median, which popped the front driver's side tire on the car. I thought, *Good, this chase is not going to last long with a blown tire; it should be easier to articulate according to policy why I was chasing the car.* The car continued to flee, even though it had a flat tire now, and turned left on to the next road, which was a major road. The car was sliding left and right as the driver attempted to steer the vehicle. Pieces of tire were flying through the air, and it was not long before sparks were flying too. The rim of the vehicle was now the only thing making contact with the concrete road.

At that point, the driver turned right at the next road, and the car went completely sideways during the turn. What was left of the tire came off the vehicle and started rolling down the street and ended up in someone's front yard. The driver decided he could not control the car so he ran it up on the curb and jumped out, beginning to run on foot. By the time I came to a stop and got out of my vehicle, he was gone.

The City Police Department showed up around this time, and we were able to set up a perimeter around the area where I last saw the guy. The department called the Garland Police Department to ask for a K9 to assist in locating the suspect. When Garland PD showed up, they asked me for a brief rundown of what happened and asked if I was able to search the subject before he ran. Once they got those answers, the officer went to his vehicle and got his dog out. He took the dog over to the vehicle, and it sniffed around. The dog immediately started sniffing the ground in a methodical fashion. Within thirty seconds, we were running after the dog, who was eager to find the suspect.

About six houses down, the dog took off between two houses. He came to the backyard fence, and there was a partially opened gate to the fence. From there, the dog went into the backyard and proceeded toward the air conditioning unit, stopped very shortly at the outside AC unit, then taking off toward the rear of the house. I looked down next to the AC unit, and that's when I saw a bag, full of white powder, that was about the size of my fist. It was cocaine.

I did not have time to pick up the bag we had just found because the dog was still running toward the rear of the house. The officers and I rounded the corner of the house and came to a wooden walkway that the owner of the house had built in the backyard. The dog continued to run toward the rear patio of the house and was barking and pulling the Garland officer harder toward the patio. That's when we found the suspect, laying between the patio and the wooden walkway. There was just enough room between the two for his body, where he was lying facedown; from there, we started giving him verbal commands. He flipped over and looked like he was trying to get up and run. That's when I heard the loudest, high-pitched scream I've ever heard from a man or woman. For a split second, the sound did not make sense; it did not match the scene. It was raw panic, high and uncontrolled. That's when we realized it came from the suspect.

The K9 officer was attempting to get his dog to back away from the suspect he was currently attacking. He was pulling on the K9's leash as hard as he could in an attempt to keep the K9 away from the suspect. The suspect was frightened and lying with his hands up. Once the dog was away from the suspect, we quickly handcuffed him. That's when we found out why the womanly scream came from the suspect: the K9 had bitten his man parts. The suspect was then taken to the hospital to get checked out for the K9 bite. Thankfully, the doctor checked him out and said he was healthy enough to go to jail, where he was charged with evading arrest and possession of cocaine.

This was the first time I had worked with a K9 and was fascinated with the encounter. I did not like the fact we had to run with the dog and keep up with him, but the K9's drive to locate the person was extraordinary. It seemed like his only goal in life was to catch the suspect, and he lived for it. However, I wondered to myself, *Why did the dog bite the suspect?* He was not running from us yet. We did not see any weapons on him. While talking to the K9 officer later, I found out the answer. Garland PD's policy was the K9 could bite the suspect if he had committed a felony, and the suspect had not been searched for weapons. No wonder the officer had asked if I was able to search the suspect; he wanted to know if he had to rein in the dog or if he could just let him do his job.

That night, I was looking for DWIs, and there were some signs of DWI before I stopped the vehicle, but that was a shaky admission. I was on shaky grounds according to policy and was worried that the department was going to have issues with the pursuit. However, they did not seem to care at all about the pursuit but were horrified about the K9 bite. The only reason I did not get in trouble for the whole thing was that it was another agency's K9 and their policies that covered them. I thought it was strange that the thing I was most worried about was of no concern to the department. I had no control over the K9, but that was the thing they were most concerned with.

This is when I started to realize there was a disconnect in the department. The department did not care about anything except the liability they assumed and how it made them look to the university. When I started, there had been officers who had been with the department for years and experienced very little turnover. It was the same way while I dispatched for them. Then one day, it felt like a light switch was turned off, and now they could not keep officers. The department was regressing toward a security force rather than a police department.

Realizing that shift changed how I felt about the job and the university I was supposed to be protecting, I stopped feeling like an asset to the department and started to feel more like a liability they were trying to manage. The pride I once felt began to erode, and was replaced by frustration and distrust. I still showed up and did work, but something fundamental had cracked, and I knew it was not going to be repaired.

ALMOST SHOOTING

I WAS WORKING THE NIGHT SHIFT ONE NIGHT AND MY friend Andrew was dispatching: he dispatched me to a burglary in progress. That was super strange, because the university never got calls like this. Andrew had received a frantic call from one of the students who said while she was in her apartment, a man whom she had never met before had come out of the bedroom and entered the living room of the apartment.

At this time, the university did not have dormitories; all the on-campus housing were apartments in which students were assigned to their own bedroom, with a common living room and kitchen area in the center of the apartment. The apartments ranged from two to four bedrooms. This apartment was on the second floor of the two-story apartment building. Lots of things were going through my mind while going to this call. How did someone enter the bedroom from a second-floor apartment? What was his intent? It was strange that there was a burglary in progress and the occupant was home, as typically burglars try and do it when no one is home so the likelihood of getting away is much better.

The caller had locked herself in a bedroom bathroom of the apartment by the time three of us officers arrived at the apartment building. We started walking up the stairs to the second-floor landing. The main door to the apartment was right at the top of the stairs to the right, with the door facing parallel to the staircase. I also noticed there was another door straight across from the staircase, which was not the main door of the apartment. Andrew was still on the phone with the caller, and the caller could still hear someone in the apartment. We told Andrew to tell the caller we were at the apartment and were going to attempt to make entry into the apartment. I checked the main door of the apartment, but it was locked.

That's when we decided to check on the off chance that maybe this bedroom door, which was perpendicular to the main door, was unlocked. I turned the door knob on the other door, and bingo, we were inside. It was pitch black in this apartment, and I could not see anything. We were trying to stay silent and make our way through this bedroom with the bed and other furniture somewhere in the room.

In training, we are taught not to use your flashlight a lot in these situations because the light restricts your pupils and takes away your night vision. It also doesn't give the suspect something to shoot at because he is in the same circumstances as you are. You don't want to give away your position by having a light on, where he could shoot at the light. Instead, you bump the on/off switch on the flashlight every so often so you can see what is there, and then you keep the light off. In the dark, unfamiliar rooms are the most dangerous. Every step had to be deliberate, every movement controlled, because a wrong turn or a rushed decision in a place like this can end a career or a life.

So here we were trying to find a way through this bedroom we had never been in before in the dark with flashlights in one hand and our guns out in the other hand. The door leading to the living room of the apartment was closed. We made our way to this door and knew that the lock for this door would be on our side so we would have direct access to the living room. We prepared ourselves to open the door and enter the living room. Another thing you need to know is that you never stay in a doorway. It prevents the officers behind you from getting in the room with you, and also if someone is going to shoot you, they are probably going to aim at the door—so you move as fast as you can to get out of the doorway.

As we ran through the door into the living room, someone bumped their light on the flashlight, and there he was. He was laying on the couch in the living room and had a pillow over his lap. All the officers started yelling at him, "POLICE! SHOW ME YOUR HANDS!" That's when he started reaching for something on his right-side waistline. What else could be he pulling on the right side of his waist but a gun? That's when I started to press the trigger while screaming, "SHOW ME YOUR HANDS!"

Things race through your mind at times like this, hundreds of thoughts in a flash. Is that really happening? What is that administration going to think? Am I going to jail? The university Police Department was not very supportive at this time of officers, questioning everything that most of the officers were doing. I knew everything was going to be looked at under a microscope and if the department could, they would hang the officer (me) out to dry. While these thoughts were racing through my head and I was screaming at the guy, the trigger was still moving toward the rear, getting close to the point of no return. From my left side, I saw a blur. One of the other officers had lunged at the guy and was tackling him.

We got him handcuffed and searched him for weapons; that's when I found out he was not armed. He had his pants unbuttoned on the couch and had been reaching his waistband with his right hand to pull up his pants. Turned out this guy actually was supposed to be a few buildings over in the same apartment at his girlfriend's apartment. He was intoxicated and had gone to the wrong apartment. I was furious! I almost killed this guy because he was intoxicated and went to the wrong apartment. He was going to jail that night, but he will never know just how close he was from being shot and changing both our lives forever. Things were on my side that night as well: if I had shot him, there is no doubt in my mind I would have lost my job and been facing criminal charges. He was taken to jail for public intoxication, and that ended that.

When I got back to the station, Andrew told me I had to hear the audio from the 911 call. Everything sounded good on the audio, calm, cool, and collected, up until he reached for his waistline. I could clearly hear on the 911 call my voice went up several octaves and screaming in a high pitch. I realized I needed to control the adrenaline rush and promised myself I would never allow things to get that close to out of control again. For several months, for no reason, Andrew would play the audio file of that 911 call again for me, and we all would have a good laugh at my expense, a lesson learned with humor.

I still think back to this incident, the way it shaped my future. The need to remain calm in all situations—I would use this as a learning opportunity forever. I was relieved that the gun did not go off; it was so close. If it would have, there is no doubt in my mind I would not have continued in law enforcement, and there was a good chance I would have been in prison. It would have been a waste of two people's lives, not because that is what I wanted to happen, but due to the actions of an intoxicated person who went out for a good time and made a mistake.

CHAPTER SEVEN

ROBBERY

I WAS WORKING ONE NIGHT THAT HADN'T BEEN PAR-
ticularly busy when the dispatcher put out a call that a robbery had
just occurred in the apartment area of the campus. The dispatcher was
able to get a description of the suspect, so I set out looking for anyone
who fit the description.

Now due to the time of night, there were not a lot of people out and
about. It was campus policing; the response time for us was under five
minutes for almost everything and on this particular night was about a
minute or so. That's super-fast and something you would not find at most
agencies, but campus policing is a niche role and if you have officers that
are wanting to do real police work and not just sit in a parking lot, quick
responses are just a part of it. The campus community as a whole wants
and needs to feel safe. The victim needed to know he was still on a safe
campus. The shaken caller was able to give general directions of travel, and
it didn't take much time to locate the suspect. He was roughly forty yards
away from me, tall, skinny, and looked pretty athletic.

As I have mentioned before, I have never been the best at running, and now I was also wearing all the gear associated with being a patrol officer. Needless to say, I did not want to chase him on foot. So, I started devising ways I could catch him if he started running. I knew I needed to stay calm. Can I catch him with my vehicle? There's a good number of cars in the parking lot, and that's not ideal because all he had to do was run between the cars and he would be in the next lane, and now I would either have to pursue him on foot or take a lot of time to find a place I could get across to the new lane.

Every option carried risk. A foot chase meant exhaustion and blind corners, while using a vehicle meant less ability to maneuver when he cut between cars. I knew that once he ran, the situation would spiral. With this realization, I needed him to stop before fear turned into distance and distance turned into something worse. Then I thought, *Can I scare him enough to comply? What's the worst that could happen? He takes off running, and I'm back to my only other options: chase on foot or chase with the car.*

So that's what I tried. I exited my vehicle and with the deepest loudest growl, I let out the words, "COME HERE!" He looked back at me and then looked the other way. I'm sure he was now contemplating his options. Much to my surprise, he started walking toward me. Inwardly, I was shocked, as I couldn't believe that worked! Once he got close, I handcuffed him. The victim was placed in a patrol vehicle, and he had another officer drive him by the suspect so the suspect would not see the victim, but the victim could see the suspect, providing the victim some safety. He was able to positively ID him as the suspect so he was arrested for robbery.

This was another lesson I learned in policing: There are several roles you have to play. Sometimes you need to be empathetic and understand where people are coming from. Sometimes you need to be stoic in sadness. Other times, you have to be bold and let out a roar, and people will respect that.

CHAPTER EIGHT

TRAFFIC DIRECTION

AT THE END OF EVERY SEMESTER, THE UNIVERSITY HAD a graduation ceremony: it was always a big day on campus. We had to all dress in our class-A uniforms with all our award ribbons and shiny buttons. The university would cater the event for all the faculty and staff that worked it, requiring all the officers to work during graduation. I had worked the night shift and now was working overtime at graduation. The graduations were always broken into several different graduations based on what degree you were getting.

They would close streets based on which parking lots were open or full; at this time, all the streets and parking lots were open. It had been a long day. I was hot and tired and ready to go home. Suddenly, I had a lady come through and tell me that her husband was right behind her. I told her that I did not know when the street was going to close, but it was open for now so be prepared for closures. She was going to the apartments on campus and not to graduation. About five minutes later, the administration decided to close the street that went through the campus. We started directing traffic away from the street since it was now closed.

By the time the husband made it to where I was, it was about ten minutes after the street had been closed. The man rolled down his window and said he had to go down that street. I said the road was closed and that he would have to go around the campus and get to the apartment. He insisted that his wife had just gone down the road, and he needed to go down it too. I told him no, and that he would have to go right, not left on the street. The man continued to protest as cars were beginning to stack up behind him. I raised my voice and said, "GO THAT WAY" and pointed to the right.

The man went and parked his car and came back to where I was. He wanted my name and badge number, which I kindly gave him a business card with all the information he wanted. The next day, he filed a formal complaint on me. Kendra was my sergeant at this time and started the investigation. She called the man, and he came in and filled out a written statement about the events that happened. They then asked me to fill out a statement about the events that morning.

The investigation looked for any policy violations that I might have made during the encounter. They asked the man if I had used any profanity or anything during the encounter, all of which he answered in the negative. I had not violated any policies and did not cuss him out. He was just upset that the street was closed, and he wanted to go that way where his wife went.

Kendra called me into her office and told me she closed the investigation and found that I had not done anything wrong. She said that although I had not broken any policy, I probably should have just let the guy do what he wanted to do and then I wouldn't have faced an investigation. This was absurd to me; what good does it do to have us directing traffic if the directions we give are just going to be ignored?

The police department did not care about the orders they had given to close the road. They just did not want any complaints and wanted to shine, no matter the implications that came with it. That day taught me it's not always my actions that would get me into trouble; it's the politics that would as well.

CHAPTER NINE

BITTEN

I WAS DISPATCHED TO A PERSON ATTEMPTING TO OVER-dose and kill themself in the parking lot of the university apartments. It was nighttime, but the parking lot lights illuminated the area. When I arrived, I saw a petite Asian female throwing hammer fists at the chest of a large male. The male could have easily stopped her, but he didn't. The thought ran through my mind that the male must be a good friend or a boyfriend of the girl and just wanted her to get help; he did not want to hurt her. I got out of my vehicle and quickly walked up to the two people. The female was screaming at the male and although my mere presence had stopped the beating the male was taking, it did not stop her yelling at him. She was crying and obviously highly emotional. Due to the circumstances, I figured this was the suicidal female call we had been dispatched to.

This looked and felt like someone I could handle without backup. I confidently grabbed both her arms and placed them behind her back. She was so petite, I was able to hold both wrists with one of my hands.

I then took out my handcuffs with the other hand and cuffed her left wrist. As soon as she felt the handcuffs hit her wrist, she started yanking away from me. I had a good hold on the handcuff wrapped around her left wrist with my left hand, so I pushed her up against the vehicle so she could not turn around on me and could not hit me with her free hand. I was attempting to pull her right hand down behind her back to secure it with the handcuff when she yanked away from me.

The woman then placed her hand in front of her and leaned over the trunk of the vehicle, effectively pinning her arm between herself and the vehicle. I was able to get my arm between her and the vehicle, and I locked onto her wrist. I began pulling her arm behind her, and it was working. She leaned to the right, placing more of her weight against the vehicle and my arm. Her efforts were in vain because I was still gaining side and backward movement of her hand; that's when I saw her head move swiftly to the right. I felt a sharp pain in my right forearm and knew she had sunk her teeth in.

Anger swelled in me in an instant. I ripped my arm from her mouth and gave a quick upper cut with my right hand to her right rib cage; that made her drop her hand by her side. I grabbed her right hand again and pulled it to me. During all this, I was not able to hold onto the cuff around her left wrist. I put my left hand on her right elbow and started pushing her elbow away from me while pulling her right wrist toward me; this is known as an arm bar, and I had a good arm bar going.

Cuffed only with one hand, I started walking her in a circular motion and at the same time saying, "Down" and pulling her toward the ground. However, she was tugging against me. I was able to shift my body position where I was facing away from her while she was still in the arm bar, avoiding getting bitten again. I told her to go down again and when she did not comply, I shifted my weight and pulled her arm. She went flying like a ragdoll and landed face first on the concrete. I landed on top of her in the chaos, and it took all the fight out of her.

I was able to then handcuff her with ease after that. When I stood up, I looked down, and there was a bluish white chunky substance, resembling cottage cheese, all down the front of my uniform. That's when I realized she had thrown up due to all the pills she had taken, and now the remnants of those pills were also all down my uniform.

EMS arrived to transport her to the hospital. While they were doing their thing and treating the female, I started looking at my forearm. There was about a quarter-sized patch of my forearm that was missing. I asked the EMS personnel if they had something to wash it out, which they gave me a bottle of water from the ambulance but provided no other treatment for me. When they were ready to take her to the hospital, they said they had to have someone ride to the hospital with them due to the combative nature of the female.

I climbed in the back of the ambulance, and we went less than two miles down the road to the nearest hospital. We entered the hospital, and the medical staff got her situated in a room. The female looked at me, and with tears running down her face, she told me she was sorry. I looked at her empathetically and said it was ok. I was thinking to myself, *I get it, you think everything is so bad in your life, you'd do anything just to die.* I knew she was in the right place to get the help she needed at the time.

Her apology stayed with me. Not because she owed me one, but because it reminded me how thin the line was between someone asking for help and someone giving up entirely. I had seen violence, anger, and chaos before, but this was different. This was the quiet desperation, and it weighed heavier than the physical pain in my arm she caused.

When the EMS personnel were about to leave, they asked for my driver's license, as they just needed to document that they looked at my forearm. I gave them my driver's license and then talked to the emergency room staff. The staff took one look at my arm and told me to follow them so they would bandage it up. They also got some paperwork, which, under the law, once filled out authorized them to check her for any communicable diseases, which she tested negative for. When they checked my blood pressure, it was super elevated and was the first time I had been told my blood pressure was high. They told me to sit down and rest as they were taking care of the female.

About thirty minutes later, they came back and took my blood pressure again, and it was still high. They seemed a little worried about how high it was and told me they weren't going to allow me to leave until my blood pressure went down. It took about an hour for my blood pressure to come down, which they said was normal for people to have elevated blood pressure after being in a fight. They set up an outpatient appointment for me to see an infectious disease doctor. About a month later, much to my surprise, I received a bill in the mail from the EMS service for the ride to the hospital.

I later learned the police administration did not like how I handled the whole situation. They never said anything to me, but they did have some other officers look at the video. They were looking at assault charges for me. I was, and still am, utterly shocked at how that administration viewed things. The lesson moving forward, though, was that nothing I did would ever be supported by these people because it seemed the important thing was not about actually enforcing the law, but the perception of the university and the public with how safe the campus was. By this stage of my career, I was naively making waves, and the administration did not like it.

CHAPTER TEN

STAPLES

I GOT IN A VEHICLE PURSUIT WITH A YOUNG MAN ONE night. It was a very short pursuit, one that did not last more than half a mile. I was sitting on a side road watching a stop sign when a vehicle never hit its brakes and went straight through the stop sign. I flipped on my lights and punched the gas pedal to get behind the vehicle. The problem was the vehicle did not pull over when he saw my lights; instead, he punched the gas. That's the moment when the adrenaline starts flowing for a cop. By policy, I was not supposed to pursue a vehicle unless it had committed a felony prior to the evading, but I had not gotten a license plate or anything other than the description of the car when he started evading me.

My thought was if I could get a plate, I might be able to catch the suspect later. I weighed the options quickly, knowing hesitation can create its own danger. The moment he chose to flee, the decision was made for me. I turned on my sirens and began the pursuit. The vehicle made a left turn onto a residential street. About the time I got close enough to the vehicle, it abruptly stopped. The suspect exited the vehicle and began running on foot. Suddenly, he slipped and fell in the front yard of a residence, and I was able to grab him and secure him in handcuffs. He had some outstanding traffic tickets he had not paid and thought he had warrants for his arrest. His decision to run increased his penalty from a fine-only offense to a felony.

There was nothing out of the ordinary about this arrest. His vehicle was towed, and I carried him down to the jail and booked him. When I got back to the police department, the jail called and said I needed to take the suspect to the hospital. I was surprised at this because when I had left the jail, everything was good, and now I had to go back to the jail and take him to the hospital. It was not totally unheard of that some people have diabetes and their sugar levels are way off, meaning you have to take them to the hospital before jail. Other people get into wrecks or have other medical issues where the jail requires you to get them medically cleared before the jail would accept them.

This one though was a first for me. When I got to the jail, the jailers told me he had hit his head on concrete walls of the jail and cut his head wide open. When I looked at him, there was only a minor cut about the middle of his forehead to his hairline. It was not a life-or-death injury, but he needed stitches or staples in his head. I transported him to the hospital, and we were placed in one of the emergency rooms. It must have taken an hour or longer before the doctor came in to treat him. The doctor was looking at his injuries when he stopped and looked at the guy.

"Haven't I seen you before?" the doctor said. The guy sheepishly nodded yes and said about a year earlier, he had been arrested by another police department. He had hit his head on the jail wall and caused his head to open the same way. He said the other police department had released him after he did that, and he had gone on about his way. I just looked at the guy and shook my head, thinking to myself, *That might work for some traffic tickets, but not when you have a felony charge for evading.*

The doctor continued to examine his head wound. After the exam was over, the doctor said he would be right back. The doctor came back with a medical staple gun. The doctor pulled the guy's hair back and cleaned the cut. He then said, "Hold on, this is going to hurt some." That's when the doctor, without adding any numbing medication or anything, began stapling this guy's head closed. I heard the click of the staple gun with every staple. The suspect squinched his face in pain. Inside, I was smiling from the instant justice that was just doled out. Just like that, it was over in less than a minute. The nurse came in with his release papers, and I took him back to jail.

This was an important lesson for me. If you're nice to your doctors and nurses, they will do a lot of things to try and make you comfortable. If you have done something stupid, they have nothing that says they have to make you comfortable before patching you up and sending you out the door.

Again, I found myself at the wrong end of the administration with this situation as well. It seemed they were angry at me again. I had gotten in a few pursuits in my career, and nothing had even been said. No verbal counseling or written reprimand. This time was different. They were looking for anything to punish me, and now they had a clear policy violation because there was not a felony committed before the pursuit. Their punishment for me was to make me take two days off for the incident, though they did allow me to use vacation time to do it instead of being non-paid.

In police culture, they will tell you if you aren't getting complained about, you're not doing your job. There's a flip side to this as well: if you are getting complained about, you're bringing attention to yourself. Most of that attention is unwanted attention. If you bring too much attention to yourself, the department looks at ways to get the attention off the department, and most of the time it's at the expense of the officer.

CHAPTER ELEVEN

HONOR KILLINGS

"HELP! HELP! MY DAD SHOT ME. MY SISTER'S ABOUT TO die, and I'm dying," a voice wailed when she called 911 asking for help. The dispatcher asks, "What's going on, ma'am?" "I'm dying, that's what's up," she said while crying.

I was working New Year's night in 2008. The shift had just started, and I received a phone call from my aunt. This was strange because I did not normally receive phone calls from her. She told me that my cousin's daughters, Amina and Sarah Said, had been found murdered in Irving, and their father had presumably murdered them. This case made international news and the girl's father, Yaser Said, was on the FBI's 10 Most Wanted list. Yaser was an Egyptian man in his thirties who married my cousin when she was fifteen. I was five or six years old when they got married so I don't have any memories of the marriage and might not have even been there. They had three children together: two daughters (Amina and Sarah) and a son (Islam).

They were at some family functions, but the family were not always present. Some of their not being around was at a young age, before they were teenagers, the girls had made accusations that Yaser had sexually assaulted them. People in my family had taken them to report it to the authorities, so Yaser stopped allowing them to be around the family. They later recanted the statements, though some of the family felt they had been pressured to recant the statements.

Here is what I have pieced together through news stories and family whispers about what happened that night. The daughters had run away and only returned at their mother's behest and lies. Yaser wanted to take them to dinner and talk about the issues. My cousin had to convince her daughter that Yaser had forgiven her before she agreed to meet with him. He pulled the trigger eleven times, riddling his daughters, one in the passenger seat and the other in the back seat of his taxi, with bullet holes. He then left them in the parking lot of a hotel in Irving, Texas; the coward then ran away. One of the daughters, Sarah, was able to use her cell phone and called 911. On the 911 recording, you can hear her beg for help that her father had just shot them. The Irving Police Department did not have an exact location for the girls, and they died in their seats of the taxi cab. Yaser disappeared after the shooting.

In the days following, I met with my cousin, her son Islam, my mother, and my sister for lunch prior to the funeral for the girls. The tension was high, and things felt really strange. All I could think in the back of my mind was that Yaser or one of his family members were going to carry out more killings at the funeral. I could not put my finger on what was wrong, but I definitely had my cop's sixth sense going. Because of that, I was not going to take any chances with my family being present.

Funerals are already charged places. Given what had occurred in their deaths, knowing the violence that had taken place, I trusted my instincts that told me this was not the place to assume everything would go smoothly. I wasn't there as a cop, but couldn't turn that part of my brain off either. So I carried two guns with me to the funeral, one in an undershirt under my left arm and the other was in my normal carry location on my right side. As we sat and talked at the restaurant, Islam made some strange statement about mischief he had gotten into while working at Wal-Mart and never graduating from school. He was proud of these things, and all I could think of was how foolish he was. The things he was proud of doing at Wal-Mart were immoral in my eyes, and it really made me think he was more involved in the murders than was generally believed.

I didn't have proof of anything. What unsettled me most was the disconnect between the gravity of the situation involving his sisters and the way he spoke about his own actions and choices. It wasn't evidence; it was instinct, the quiet alarm I'd learned not to ignore over the years in law enforcement.

When we arrived at the funeral home, I noticed some men walking around the outside of the funeral home. The funerals were stopped in the middle of the service due to some outrage from Islam about the funeral, as he was mad about the Christian versus Islamic funeral proceedings.

After the funeral, I went back to my apartment and called the Irving Police Department, offering to assist in any manner I could. I wanted them to find the killer and for him to face the punishment that was due him. The officers asked me for some family history, which I told them I would get for them. I had to call my Aunt Gail to get some of the information they were asking for because I was too young to remember the details. After that, they never contacted me again, but they did speak directly to Aunt Gail. At some point, the FBI got involved because one of the theories was that Yaser had fled to his home country of Egypt.

Years passed with more questions than answers, and the unease I felt never went away. What I noticed back then stayed with me, unresolved until the truth finally surfaced much later. In 2018, Yaser was apprehended at a house in Justin, Texas; his brother and Islam were charged with aiding and abetting a fugitive for their parts in Yaser's escape from prosecution. Yaser was convicted of the murders of his daughters, while Islam pleaded guilty to aiding his father.

For many years, this case caused strain in the family. Some of the family wanted to be supportive of my cousin and her family, while the others wanted them charged along with the actual killer as co-conspirators. For me, I just did not want anything to do with my cousin or her son after that. There was even a Christmas where I stayed at work instead of having anything to do with them, hiding the fact that I did not come home because my cousin was there. I did not want to miss Christmas and my family, but I could not bring myself to be in the same house with a person I partially blamed for the murders of her daughters.

CHAPTER TWELVE

TWENTY-SECOND BIRTHDAY

I WAS PATROLLING AROUND 2 A.M. WHEN I SAW A VEHI-cle doing 58 mph in a 40-mph zone. With a U-turn, I caught up to the vehicle and initiated a traffic stop on the vehicle by turning on the emergency red and blue lights. At this time of the night, you always suspect the person might be intoxicated (as I shared earlier in the book). After stopping, I approached the driver and started my traffic stop. The smell of an alcoholic beverage coming from the vehicle hit me in the face. However, the driver informed me he was the designated driver for the passenger, who was celebrating his twenty-second birthday since he did not get to celebrate his twenty-first birthday. The driver and passenger were both students and lived at the apartments on campus.

When I looked at the passenger, there was vomit from his mouth to his knees. He was not moving, and his head was hanging down against the window of the vehicle. I attempted to talk to the passenger while the driver tried to shake him awake. The driver said he was speeding, trying to get the guy to his apartment so he would stop puking in his vehicle. This statement irked me, as I felt like the driver was unconcerned for his friend's health. They had driven by a hospital, and he was just going to put his friend to bed in the condition he was in.

The drinking did not bother me; it was the indifference of the man's friend. I had already seen enough to know this wasn't someone who just needed to sleep. Leaving him like that wasn't careless; it was dangerous. I walked around the car and opened the passenger door, shaking the guy harder, trying to get some response from him. The guy did not move. I radioed to dispatch and asked them to send an ambulance to my location for an intoxicated person. While the ambulance was en route, I attempted to wake the passenger up and even rubbed my knuckles across the sensitive skin on the chest, performing a sternum rub on him to awaken him. It's not comfortable and wakes almost everyone up when you do it, unless they have some serious medical issues. I knew this guy needed some help immediately when he didn't respond and was glad I was there to give it to him.

When the ambulance arrived, they loaded the unconscious passenger on the stretcher and took him to the hospital. I then turned my attention back to the driver, doing field sobriety tests on him to make sure he was not intoxicated. Once I was satisfied that he was telling the truth about being the designated driver and not drinking, I issued him a ticket for speeding. I felt like he did not care that his friend was in such dire condition; he just wanted him to stop puking in his car. The ticket would be a little reminder of the lack of judgment he made that night.

The next day when I came to work, I asked if there was any update on the condition of the passenger. I was told he was in the intensive care unit and that if I had not stopped that vehicle, he would have probably died because he had aspirated. A couple days went by, and the captain spoke to me. He was mad that I gave the driver of the vehicle a ticket for speeding. I tried to explain that he was doing 18 mph over the speed limit, he had passed the hospital, and he was just going to put his friend in bed without proper care. We would have had a dead student on our hands. The captain dismissed all my reasons and chewed me out for writing up the driver. My sergeant put me in for a commendation for saving the life of the student which the captain reduced to a letter of recognition.

I was very confused about the whole thing. I saved someone's life, but the only thing the administration wanted to focus on was the speeding ticket I gave his friend. I was out trying to be the best police officer I could be but nothing I did was good enough. I did not see any of the other officers getting treated like this, so it felt like they had a personal problem with me. There was no policy violation, but the administration were always going to find something that I did wrong. This caused me to start looking for employment at other departments soon after the incident.

CHAPTER THIRTEEN

HURRICANE IKE

IN SEPTEMBER OF 2008, HURRICANE IKE DEVASTATED the island of Galveston. The university component located in Galveston asked for officers from the other components to come and assist them during the cleanup efforts. Two officers from my component were sent every week for three weeks to Galveston to assist them. There was a fear that things might get violent in the area like the not-too-distant Hurricane Katrina in New Orleans, and they wanted to be prepared for it. I volunteered to go and was placed in the second week of officers to assist them.

We left for Galveston on a Sunday morning, and the drive down was peaceful like any other Sunday stroll until we got to the bridge crossing into Galveston Island. There were boats strewn across the bridge; that was an incredibly powerful sight. These weren't small boats that you see on the lakes but ocean vessels. What type of power must this storm have to lift these boats two or three stories and toss them like ragdolls onto the bridge?

I sat in the seat of the vehicle trying to understand the scale of what I was seeing. It was an overwhelming scene. When we entered the island, all the buildings were boarded up, and there were piles stretching the whole length of every street with furniture and rubble from the water-logged buildings. I was overwhelmed with the sight of the destruction I was seeing. They put us in the San Luis Resort, a four-star award-winning hotel. When we entered the hotel, the smell of mold and mildew permeated the air; it was a smell we would get used to during our stay for the next three weeks.

They wanted to place an officer at every door to the university twenty-four hours a day, with every officer having a patrol rifle to secure the buildings, but they did not want you to have a round in the chamber. It was overkill, though, as you never saw a person besides another officer at night. By not allowing a round in the chamber, it symbolized the system as a whole. It looked like a regular police department, but it was not ready to walk and talk like a real police department. I was assigned to night shift to monitor the surrounding area, and this was the first time I had ever seen a curfew imposed where no one was allowed to be outside after 8 p.m. The school also had assignments patrolling some of the other outlining properties that the university owned, and you got your assignment at the shift briefing on the evening when you showed up.

On one shift I was assigned with an officer from the university to patrol some of their other buildings. The officer was able to convey to me things that happened during the storm, telling me stories about the building we were patrolling along with stories about the island itself. He recounted to me how they all had to stay during the storm and said it was a scary venture during the storm. The officer mentioned that they unwisely stayed in rooms that all had windows to the outside and said if they had been smarter, they would have put their beds in the hallways and avoided the windows. The stories he told about the island itself were mostly ghost stories. Galveston is supposed to be one of the most haunted places in Texas.

For example, we were patrolling one of the houses that was donated to the university by a wealthy family on the island, and the officer was telling me about the rumors of the house being haunted. All of a sudden, there was a loud crash in the house. We were freaked out by the noise. No one was supposed to be out because of the curfew, and we had not seen or heard anyone but ourselves for several hours. We both drew our guns and proceeded to search the house for wherever or whoever caused the crash sound. After thoroughly combing through every inch of that house, we were unable to locate anything that was out of place. We chalked it up to ice having dropped from a commercial icemaker located in the kitchen area.

Looking back, Hurricane Ike was more than just a storm; it was a preview of the storm about to hit my career in law enforcement. Patrolling the city on lockdown and chasing shadows in a house we swore was haunted, I learned to live with tension, uncertainty, and the sense that something bigger than me could rip my life apart. I didn't know it then, but the real storm was waiting for me back at my department.

CHAPTER FOURTEEN

PROMOTION AND FIRING

THE YEAR 2008 WAS A PIVOTAL YEAR FOR ME, AS I CLIMBED and I crashed. By the end of the year, I would get promoted, experience Hurricane Ike's brutal aftermath on Galveston, and experience a personal hurricane ripping through my career.

The excitement of being a cop at the university PD had started to wane by this time, and I was looking for employment at other police departments in the area. There was a lot of movement within the police department because several people were unsatisfied working there. You never saw the command staff; they always stayed tucked into their offices and were disconnected from the rest of the employees.

Meanwhile, I was out making a statement with DWI arrests. At least one other officer joined me in my efforts, and I was starting to get some heat for them. There was some murmuring about issues with my number of DWIs from the police administration, and they started looking at the locations of my traffic stops. The student affairs office was having to deal with tons of students getting DWIs, as one of the fraternities was getting suspended from activities due to their parties on and off campus. Due to the relative unease at the department, the vice president of business affairs (think city manager) held a meeting with all the members of the department to get our feedback.

I was pretty vocal about some of the issues causing problems for patrol. Unfortunately, the chief of police in this meeting acted like everything was going well, and there were no problems. I raised issues with our equipment, mainly patrol vehicles, because we had not gotten a new vehicle since I started. Instead, they had bought "low mileage" used patrol vehicles. Now go ask any cop if they would buy a used patrol vehicle, and I bet ninety-nine percent, or maybe even every officer you talk to, will tell you it's not a good idea, yet this was the equipment we were working with.

It was 2008, and you mostly could not find a patrol vehicle without a computer in the vehicle, as the technology had advanced beyond mobile data terminals. Unfortunately, we still did not have either in our vehicles, and there were no plans to even look at getting them. I made this issue known to the vice president. The vice president looked at the chief and asked if this was correct, which she answered in the affirmative. He then told her to look into getting computers and new vehicles.

I'm pretty sure I stepped on some toes in that meeting, but we were told that's what they wanted, and I was too naïve to know better, but it seemed the administration started looking at ways to get me. Despite the new computers in the new vehicles, it did not help the overall management of the police department. I started turning in applications for other departments in the area. Every time I turned around, I was being questioned about the amount of traffic stops I was making off campus, and they wanted to contain the traffic stops to the campus. The way I took this is that I was costing the school money arresting its students for DWIs, and they wanted to stop me from doing DWIs, so they were trying to contain me and make me less effective.

I realize now that good police work does not always align with good politics. I was not being questioned because I was doing something wrong; I was being questioned because I was doing too much of something right.

My sergeant at the time was having me put the location of where I observed the traffic offense in the dispatch notes, even though by the time I caught up to the vehicles, they were often on one of the side streets surrounding the campus. He wanted to make a log that was trackable to show that I was on campus when I saw the offense. I also received several letters of recognition during this time for my work. The strangest thing was that my chain of command had put me in for commendations (highest-level award) for me, but when it went to the captain, he would always drop it down to a letter of recognition (the lowest award). The same captain once told me the commendation I had received for making DWI arrests was the worst thing he ever allowed to happen. I felt like he did not want me doing police work and just wanted campus security with the police name.

There was an opening for a corporal position at the university PD, and I wanted the position because I thought at the time that I had skills the department wanted and needed. I was also disillusioned with the department I worked at and felt like it was time to move to another department. Soon, I received a phone call from the patrol commander saying I would get the corporal position as long as I withdrew from the hiring process at the other department. I asked for the salary scale they were offering and was told $49,000 per year. I asked the patrol to put it in writing, since the chief was known for offering you one thing and doing something else. He wrote me the email, and I withdrew from the hiring process at the other department. They promoted two people to corporal under the $49,000 pay I was quoted.

I understood that the department needed confirmation that I would not soon leave the department, and offering the higher pay was their incentive to make it happen. I didn't regret the outcome, but I clearly saw how conditional loyalty could be.

Later, I was told when the pay was being calculated, the chief had planned on promoting us at a much lower rate but was stopped when she was told I had gotten the offer in writing. I was also told she said something to the effect that people would pay for that.

They hired two officers to fill the vacancies from the promotions, and I was tasked as one of the FTOs for both the new hires; they both had previous law enforcement experience. The way I looked at things, everyone was a rookie while they were on FTO, and I used the language as such. One day at the beginning of the shift, the patrol commander overheard me calling one of the guys a rookie and called me into his office, telling me to stop using that language.

Later, while we were riding around that evening, I told the guy I was training that I had to stop using the word rookie for him. Nothing was further said about it throughout training until the last day of FTO for the two guys. University PD had implemented a check ride with the patrol commander before being released from FTO.

The next day was an off day for me, and I had set up with some of the other guys to go golfing at a golf course in McKinney. I was playing golf with my third phase FTO, who had moved on to another department, and some of my coworkers. While golfing, I received a phone call telling me I needed to come to the PD immediately. So I packed up my gear and drove to the police department.

I walked into the department not knowing why I had been called back in. I had no reason to believe that I was in trouble because my focus had always been on the streets and the job itself. I hadn't learned to watch my words the way I watch the suspects.

That's when I was told they were going to demote me back to officer for calling the new guys rookies. I would have thought it would be a suspect that would get the best of me, not the interoffice politics and the use of one little word. They claimed that the word "rookie" was demeaning to a new officer; to me, it felt less about protecting the new officer and more about enforcing a version of professionalism that I didn't recognize.

It just so happened that one of my good friends was an attorney who specialized in police employment matters and worked with the Texas Municipal Police Association (TMPA). I had joined TMPA while I was a dispatcher for the legal protections they offered. I had never used their services before and hadn't thought I would need it unless someone sued me for a law enforcement action I had taken against them. Before I pulled out of the parking lot, I had already made a phone call to my friend, and he showed up at the office when I had a meeting later that day with the chief of police to get my formal demotion letter. My friend advised me to come to his office and bring my policy manual with me the next day.

He then sent a reply to the demotion, telling them all the things they did wrong with the demotion. The biggest thing was the law required an investigation into the facts before you could demote a police officer.

Needless to say, they called me back into the office, reinstated me back to corporal, but they reassigned me to day shift. I have been told in the next day or so that they talked to several officers and asked about anything I did that they could use against me. A few days later I was brought back into the office and was now facing several other administrative charges they were investigating. They asked me about a traffic stop I had done while training one of the guys. Particularly they wanted to know the speed I was going to make the traffic stop.

This was a six-lane road with a center median dividing the lanes. It was late at night so there were almost no vehicles on the road. The speed limit on this road was 45 mph. Due to the median, you would have to drive several blocks before you could make a U-turn and go catch up to the vehicle. I did not want to allow the vehicle to get too far away from campus seeing that I was already getting messed with for doing traffic stops off campus. So I drove much faster than I would normally have to in order to make this traffic stop; in excess of 100 mph. When they asked me how fast I was going I answered that I did not know the exact speed, but I was going very fast.

Little did I know, that statement was going to be construed as a lie. They grilled me about the speed I was going and every time I told them I did not know the exact speed, but it was very fast. That's when they started asking me if it was over 80 mph? Which I responded with a yes head nod and said yes, probably. 90 mph? Again, a head nod. And probably 100 mph? And again a yes, a head nod, and the word "probably." I reiterated that I did not know the exact speed I was going. They told me the guy I was training said I was going 104 mph to make that traffic stop and asked if I had any reason to not believe he was correct with the speed. I told them I had no reason to not believe him and if he said I was doing 104 then I was probably doing 104, but I did not know the exact speed. They called me a liar. They wrote more complaints against me to that effect and made me take a polygraph to prove that I was not lying. According to their polygraph person I had lied during the investigation. They then terminated me for lying in an administrative investigation.

I found myself in a daze. Is this really happening? How did it get to this point? I was being escorted out of a job which I had worked at for more than six years. This was November of 2008. I had just been dismissed from my role as a corporal with the university Police Department. I was twenty-six years old. My first employment with a job outside of the family business had been with this police department and now here I am being walked out.

My lawyer friend had been keeping tabs on the incident since my first phone call to him. I called him back and gave him the update and again he had me come to his office. There we wrote a response to the termination which again pointed out several violations which had occurred with their investigation. In the response letter which he crafted and had me read over and sign if I agreed, there was a small error or miswording in the statement. I don't remember exactly what it was now, I should have gotten him to correct that statement, but I didn't. I signed the response to the termination and we turned it into the university PD.

I was again called into the office and reinstated as corporal, but they then placed me on administrative leave pending another investigation. This time, they had the system agency do the investigation, adding the charges of turning the camera system off too soon after the stop, conduct unbecoming an officer, failure of a supervisor to provide an example, and so on, to the investigation. I knew deep down it was all over, but I was going to fight them all the way. The investigation took over a month to complete, and I had not seen another officer try to fight the system as we did. They all just left the department and moved on to other things, but I decided to stay and fight the system.

I spent the first week or two on leave just lying in bed. I was confused, shocked, and in a state of disbelief that all of this had spiraled to this point. I was still getting paid as though I was working every day, but the only thing I could not do was work. My cousin had a flexible job, and he was into smoking cigars, so I ended up spending my days hanging out with my cousin and smoking cigars. I also started drinking pretty heavily at this time, as I had nothing to do. I was in limbo. I couldn't apply for other jobs, couldn't go to work. I felt stuck.

The silence made it worse. No calls, no purpose. The job had always told me who I was and where I belonged; without it, the days blurred together. Drinking and smoking weren't a relief but ways to make time pass. I was not resting. I was waiting.

The system department sent an inspector from Austin to investigate the case, as they were going to make sure they dotted their I's and crossed their T's in this investigation. The way they ordered me to do the first polygraph test made the test invalid, so they sent me to do another polygraph test. This time, they said I passed the polygraph test, which gave me hope that I wouldn't be terminated after all.

Then, in mid-December 2008, my third-phase FTO, Terry McCurry, committed suicide. I never knew Terry was battling his own demons as he seemed like the perfect cop and someone to strive toward. His suicide made me realize that even the best could be broken. At the time, I didn't know what to do with that realization. I was already unraveling, and losing someone I looked up to felt like confirmation that none of us were as solid as we pretended to be in law enforcement.

A week later, I received a letter in the mail stating the department was terminating me again. This time, the word termination did not crush me like it had before. It ended up that the one thing I had caught that my attorney had written in the rebuttal letter was the thing that ended up hanging me. This was no fault of the attorney, as I had caught the mistake and did not do anything about it. I can not remember exactly what it was, but it was a small error and just needed to be worded differently.

Up until this point in my career, I had always trusted the system and knew the system was not perfect, but everyone seems to think it was the best system in the world. However, the system failed me, and now I was left to figure out how I was going to move forward from here. I thought the badge was a shield, but in the end, it cut me down.

I was broken.

CHAPTER FIFTEEN

WRECKER DRIVER

I SPENT THE MONTH OF DECEMBER IN A DAZE AND NOT really doing much. When the new year arrived, I set out looking for a new job. I felt tired of police work and wanted a fresh start. I also wanted to start attending church again; I had let that slip and was not following any of the teachings I knew needed to be followed as a Christian. Sadly, my drinking started getting worse.

Meanwhile, the chief at the university Police Department had her own dirty laundry aired in the most public way. It was mentioned in the Dallas news, and she was placed on administrative leave, ended up resigning during that period of time. The whole command staff also resigned during this period.

So, 2008 was a tough year for all. There was a banking crisis in the United States at the same time, and the economy was still trying to recover. Jobs were tough to come by, and there seemed to be plenty of competition for the jobs that were available. I did not want to do policing full time, but I wanted to still hold onto my license from the state. The chief of police of the city where my friend worked, which I wrote about earlier, offered me a reserve police officer position within his department, which I took. Yes, the same department with the hanging scarecrow. I was able to feed my need for an adrenaline rush of policing, and it kept the desire for the job alive.

I was working day shift, mid-day to evening time frame. This was a sleepy town that normally rolled up the sidewalks at 10 p.m. One night, I was sitting in my patrol vehicle in the downtown area when a car pulled up beside me. They told me about a vehicle driving erratically and speeding. I told them I would keep an eye out for the vehicle, but in the back of my mind, I was thinking there was no way I was ever going to be able to find this vehicle. They did not even have a direction of travel to go with on this vehicle.

Just a few minutes had passed while I was still watching the stop sign in the center of downtown. I decided to move and drive around just so I could say I looked for that vehicle. I pulled out of the area I was parked at and began to drive. I remember thinking it would be a nothing call, the kind you forget by the end of the shift. Then, I looked in my rearview mirror and noticed a car approaching me fast and when I said fast, it was at least 20 mph over the speed limit. The car never slowed down. Here I was driving a marked police vehicle and instead of attempting to avoid me like most people do, the vehicle passed me in a no-passing zone.

It's the kind of call that should have ended with a citation, but something just didn't fit. People slow down when they see a police vehicle. This driver didn't hesitate, didn't acknowledge me at all. I attempted to make a traffic stop on the vehicle, but it just ignored me. It ran a stop sign without even looking to see if other cars were present. We were headed out of the city limits into some farmland.

The driver turned off the main road and started down a road surrounded by pastures. When we came to an old farm and barn, the vehicle turned into the driveway and started heading toward the barn. We drove through the open barn doors and came out the other side through another open barn door. The vehicle continued to drive erratically and went into the field. Just like that, the vehicle stopped. I ordered the driver out of the vehicle at gunpoint, who was a woman, and handcuffed her.

That's when I found out there were three kids in the vehicle, varying in age from early teens down to five or six years old. The driver was their mother. On closer inspection of the vehicle, I noticed barbed wire fence wire had been wrapped through the roof of the vehicle and the front windows. At that, I asked the driver about the barbed wire and she said it was there to protect them. She also said she was carrying some anointing olive oil in her bra, saying she was attempting to find a water well in the area where the evil spirits were telling her to throw her kids into the water well.

I was shocked. This woman was about to kill her children, and I just happened to be in the right place at the right time to stop it. I took her to jail to book her for evading arrest and child endangerment. However, the jail refused her and said she needed medical clearance first due to her mental health. So I took her to the hospital. We had to sit at the hospital and wait for them to call for a screening. It was a couple hours' wait until someone showed up to do the screening. The screener came out of the room and said she was one of the worst cases she had ever seen, saying she needed to go to a behavioral hospital, so I left her in the custody of the hospital.

The reserve police officer position was unpaid, and I needed to find something to pay the bills. I found a towing company that was looking for drivers, so I interviewed with them and was hired. They towed for several city police departments around the Dallas area, including the Dallas Police Department. They also did a lot of business with car dealerships across the area.

The thing about being a tow truck driver, at least at this place, was you worked long hours. It was twelve hours a day, Monday-through-Friday job. On top of that, you were required to be on call every other night and every other weekend. The weeks you worked Tuesday and Thursday nights on call, you would have those weekends off. The weeks you worked Monday, Wednesday, and Friday nights on call, you would also work the weekends. Needless to say, it was not uncommon to work over a hundred hours in a week. There was even a time when I went to work on Friday morning and only got 30 minutes to an hour sleep from then until Monday night at 7 p.m. This company also did not have any benefits for the employees. No healthcare, no paid time off, and if you took time off, you had to find another driver who was willing to cover your on-call nights and weekends.

Not having healthcare proved to be a tricky thing with this job. There was a time when I was driving down an interstate when another car spun out on a water puddle. The vehicle hit me head on while I was in a wrecker working. My hand swelled due to the wreck, and I did not have money at the time to have the surgery to fix my hand, so I have some nerve damage in my left hand, which makes my pinky finger numb. Fifteen years later, I still have the numb pinky.

Another time I was running a fever and attempted to call in sick. They made me come to work anyway, which angered me so I spent all the time I could in the boss's office, coughing and just feeling miserable. Finally, he told me to go home. I worked this job for almost three years, both loving and hating that job all at the same time. There was no way I could make a career out of it with the insane number of hours and no benefits.

One of my high school friends became a supervisor for a roofing company and offered me a spot in the company. It was lower pay, but it had a regular schedule, so I jumped at the opportunity. This would allow me time with friends and family and the opportunity to regularly attend church.

After months of chaos, the predictability mattered more than the paycheck. Knowing where I would be each day, when I would be home each day, and that I could plan a week instead of surviving one gave me something I hadn't had in a long time: stability. That routine didn't fix everything, but steadied me enough to start paying attention to things I'd been too busy to see before.

My friends were going to church too, and we were making plans together to make sure we did not miss a service. We were getting involved with the church and serving others to where God was a central figure in my life. I felt God's love for me like I had never felt it before during this time. Things were looking up. Little did I know that in less than three months, the company was going to go out of business and I was not going to have a job again. I thought I had found stability; instead, I was back to zero, but this time, I was not walking alone.

In that three-month time, I really dug into my faith, which was what pulled me through the failure of not being employed again. I was looking into ways I could still be in the police world but not be a full-time officer. I even contemplated looking into police chaplaincy and doing things that would benefit officers who felt the crushing weight of the world on their shoulders. However, I was not really ready for that yet. I still needed to work on myself and grow more in my faith, but there was a pull deep down inside me that I needed to help other first responders, and it was not long before I would find my next step.

CHAPTER SIXTEEN

LAMAR UNIVERSITY PD

I WAS IN THE MIDDLE OF MY INTERVIEW FOR THE LAMAR University Police Department. I went to speak during the interview, and all of a sudden, my voice was coming out of my mouth as soft and raspy. I could not believe this was happening. This might be my best opportunity at a full-time job in police work, and now I felt that I looked weak and helpless. I don't know why my voice went away, and I haven't had it happen since.

I wanted to get back into full-time police work. I missed the job, the paycheck, the pension and insurance you get working for the government. In late 2011, someone I knew from my involvement with the Police Explorers got hired as the chief of police for Lamar University. I messaged him and inquired about where he thought my chances were in ever getting hired back full time as a police officer. He told me it would be hard work for me, but he did not think necessarily that I would be unhireable. I was encouraged by this; with my previous attempts at getting hired, I had serious doubts about whether

I would ever be able to be a full-time police officer again. I was attending church every Sunday and was growing in my relationship with God, praying to Him to open doors for me.

Around November 2011, the chief of police posted five new positions he was hiring at Lamar Police Department in Beaumont, Texas. I applied for one of the positions, even though it was five hours from the Dallas area where I was living; this was because I was not having any luck in the Dallas area of finding a police department to work for with my background. I was thinking that moving to an area where no one knew me might be a fresh start, a new beginning. Thankfully, I was called and given an interview date.

Getting this interview felt like a breakthrough, but I had learned not to confuse opportunity with outcome. I also kept praying for God to open the right place for me, trusting Him regardless of whether this was a door opening or closing. Either way, I would still be standing on the other side.

When making the journey from Dallas to Beaumont, the closer I got to Beaumont, the more trees lined the highway. Immediately, I was drawn to the area and the forest surrounding it. I have always loved the mountains and trees, and this area had one of the two elements I loved, including several national forests and national preserves, where I was able to observe, firsthand, the beauty of God's design.

I arrived early for my interview, and as it was the first time I had ever been to the area, I drove around. In the neighborhood surrounding Lamar, I saw a lot of people just standing around outside their houses drinking 40 oz. beers. The smell of weed was everywhere. This was perplexing; it was a weekday and approaching the lunch hour, so why were people not at work? What caused several people in the area to be drinking at such an early time in the day? The houses in the area looked old and decrepit. Several of the houses were boarded up and looked like the slightest breeze might push them over. When I thought about crime-riddled neighborhoods, the neighborhood surrounding Lamar was what I pictured.

In the meantime, I sat down for the interview. Even though my voice failed me, in mid-December, I got the call and was offered a position and a new start at Lamar University Police Department, with a start date of January 2, 2012. This time in my life had a lot of mixed emotions. I was excited to get back into full-time policing, and it was a fresh beginning in an area I had really no close friends and no family. I was having to figure out living arrangements in the next two weeks in the middle of the Christmas season. It seemed like there was so much to do in such a short time, but help was coming. I was, and still am, so grateful to the assistant chief for opening up his guest house for a few days just to give me some time to figure it all out. I was hopeful that I had found somewhere where I could make a life and career.

CHAPTER SEVENTEEN

FTO AT LAMAR

THE CRIME IN THE SOUTH END OF BEAUMONT, WHERE Lamar University is located, was the worst I'd experienced thus far, and I loved every minute of it. It was pure chaos in the neighborhood surrounding Lamar. Drugs, alcohol, and gangs were abundant. The goal of the chief of police for Lamar University was to clean up the area surrounding Lamar so the crime would not spill over to the campus, so I spent most of my time working in the surrounding neighborhoods and not on the campus itself. PCP was a big drug in the neighborhood. On a weekend night, it was a slow night if you weren't dealing with three or four people, all of whom were on PCP. Crack cocaine was also big in the area, and it felt like everyone was smoking marijuana.

Every time you go to a new police department, you have to start with field training. While in FTO at Lamar University during my first few weeks of working there, Lamar PD got with the Beaumont Street Crimes unit for a weekend of heavy enforcement in the neighborhoods surrounding Lamar. I made a traffic stop in the neighborhood and was approaching the vehicle on the driver's side while my FTO was approaching on the passenger side. About the time we got to the vehicle, there was a loud *POP* sound, which we immediately knew was gunfire.

For a moment, everything, including us, froze. We didn't speak, just looked at each other and checked to make sure the other was okay and still standing. In a split second, we were facing our own mortality. Once we knew both of us were okay, it was time to go to work. Unfortunately, we did not know where the gunshot came from and if it was aimed at us. We knew it did not come from the vehicle we had stopped so we told them they were free to go. The FTO and I started looking for people around us where the shots might have come from. Ultimately, we never found where the gunfire came from, but that was the first time I had ever felt like I had been possibly shot at.

My second-phase FTO turned out to be a good friend of mine over time. He was a young cop and had only been in law enforcement for about a year and a half. He was really high-strung and by the book, while I had ten years of experience, seven of them as a police officer. He was a go-getter like I was, but he was green. We were driving when I observed an eighties model Cadillac headed the opposite direction from me. It was dark at this point in the evening and when I looked in my side mirror, I noticed the vehicle did not have any tail lights. I slammed on my brakes and went to make a U-turn. My FTO looked over at me and asked what I was doing. I told him, "You'll see," trying to match his cockiness with my confidence and prove I knew what I was doing.

It wasn't as much arrogance as awareness. After years on the job, you start noticing what doesn't fit, the vehicles that don't match the scene, the drivers that don't react the way most people do when they see a patrol car. The car was just off. I stopped the vehicle for not having tail lights. While I was talking to the driver, he was super nervous. At one point, I asked him for consent to search the vehicle, which he gave me. While searching the vehicle, I located over a pound of marijuana in the driver's door; he went to jail for possession of marijuana.

At the jail, my FTO asked how I knew to stop that vehicle. I shrugged and told him it was a sixth sense.

I did my first DWI at Lamar PD while on second-phase FTO. Like my previous University PD, Lamar PD almost never did DWIs, and Lamar was a prime area for working DWIs. There were a couple clubs just down the street, including a topless bar. At Lamar, it wasn't anything for me to arrest 2–3 DWIs a week and unlike the university Police Department, I never had to go to court on any of the DWIs I did at Lamar PD.

Another time with the second-phase FTO, I had made a traffic stop on a vehicle and immediately smelled the odor of marijuana, which due to a Supreme Court ruling, allows you to search a vehicle without a warrant. I immediately got the driver out of the vehicle and handcuffed him; my FTO did the same to the passenger. Once they were handcuffed, the FTO asked me what I was doing, which I told him to watch and learn, proceeding with everything needed to charge someone with marijuana. Toward the end of my second-phase FTO, the FTO was being very 'by the book' about something when I looked over at him and told him he needed to chill out or take a Xanax or something.

Was I being arrogant? Well, a little, but I knew he thought he knew more than he actually knew, and I was going to make a point to him that other people knew just as much if not more than he did. I felt like I had to make him feel like we were equals and that I had enough confidence to where I did not need to be in training anymore. It was a bold move, and it paid off. Soon after that, I was released from field training, having completed it.

My second-phase FTO later told me he knew I knew my stuff and that I had more experience than he had. He was learning more from me and was scared that he might mess up. After I told him he needed a Xanax, he knew right then he was either going to hate me or we were going to be lifelong friends. It turned out to be the latter.

In moments like the first time we heard gunfire, which could have been at us, it's hard to feel the emotions of the moment. You learn through your career to suppress emotions, not because emotions are good or bad, but they get in the way of duty. Time is of essence in the heat of battle and taking the time for emotions slows you down, and that slowdown could cost you your life. Sometimes you don't ever unpack all the suppressed emotions; the suppression just becomes another day. No one is perfect, and we have all failed. My inner peace and strength comes from the knowledge that even though we all are sinners, Jesus died on the cross for not only my sins, but for every single one of our sins. It's an amazing grace that we are not worthy to receive. The redemption I had been given going to Lamar felt like a small piece of the redemption received from Jesus.

CHAPTER EIGHTEEN

POLICING AT LAMAR

I HAD ONLY BEEN WORKING AT LAMAR UNIVERSITY PD for a couple months, but I was off of FTO almost right away. In a regular shift, it was about 9 p.m., and we were dispatched to a robbery in progress. I raced to the area in my patrol vehicle, learning that the student being robbed was in the parking lot of the school when he was surrounded by three men who wanted to take his wallet. He did not give it to them, and they jumped him, running away soon after. I was driving through the neighborhood, looking for any signs of the men who just robbed the student. Then, I noticed a man ducking into the backyard of a house.

I made my way to the house and started searching for the man I saw. My heart was pounding, and I was trying to control the adrenaline that was coursing through my veins. From there, I crept through the backyard so no one would hear me approach. I would only turn on my flashlight in the shadow areas of the backyard where it was pitch black. That's where I saw a shed, which had about a foot between it and the fence. I turned on my flashlight in that dark section between the shed and the fence and there he was, lying face down on the ground, trying to hide.

I pointed my gun at him and began giving him the orders. "Show me your hands, turn around, and face away from me!" He was complying with my orders, but he kept putting his hands down. I was worried that he was going to go for a gun or some other weapon that he had secreted away in the front of his pants. This guy had just committed a robbery, and having a gun is especially concerning because he probably had one to rob the student. I firmly and confidently told him if he put his hands down again, I was going to kill him.

I didn't say it out of anger. I said it because he kept reaching and I needed him to understand, without any ambiguity, what the next move would cost him. With every word I spoke, I pressed that gun toward him. I wanted to convey to him I was deadly serious, while concealing the fact that I was shaking from fear and the adrenaline rush. He whimpered to me that he had been stabbed. I reassured him that I would deal with that in a minute, and he needed to keep his hands up.

I told dispatch I had one person at gunpoint, and he advised he had been stabbed and to send me an ambulance. At this point, I didn't exactly know how this man was connected to the scene, but all the signs pointed to him. I handcuffed the man and asked him where he had been stabbed, to which he told me his chest. I lifted his shirt and saw a puncture wound just above his right nipple. I did not know the size of the knife that he was stabbed with, and there was barely any blood to let you even know he had been stabbed. I wondered if the blood was pooling internally rather than externally. The ambulance arrived and began treating the suspect; this was all happening very quickly. They loaded him into the ambulance and were off to the hospital within the first five minutes of arriving on scene. I rode in the ambulance with the suspect to the hospital. The ambulance had its lights and sirens on as we headed to the hospital. He was lucky that the knife did not hit any of his vital organs. After a couple hours at the hospital, he was taken to jail for robbery.

What I would learn later was the student had just gotten out of the Marine Corps, where he served in Force Recon, the Marines Special Forces unit. He had made himself a promise when he left the Marine Corps that he was never going to kill someone again. These three men forced him to make a choice to betray himself or allow himself to use the skills he had already honed in battle to protect himself. When these men grabbed this student, the Force Recon Marine came out in him. He grabbed his pocket knife and started stabbing the guys. One of the guys had grabbed him from the rear, putting his arm around his neck, which the Marine stabbed him in the arm that was wrapped around his neck. The other guy attempted to grab the Marine's arm and take his knife. The Marine stabbed this suspect in the chest; this was the suspect I found hiding in the back-yard of the house. The third guy wanted no part of getting stabbed, and all three ran away.

The Marine didn't look like a victim or suspect. He looked like someone who had been forced back into a life he thought he'd left be-hind. He survived, but I knew there was a cost to that kind of survival.

We apprehended all the suspects, and they all went to jail. As with most cases, I don't know the outcome from the arrests: maybe they pled guilty, maybe the charges were dropped. All I know is I was never called to testify in court about the incident. I have often wondered what ever became of the Marine.

During this time, I was learning fast that policing here was differ-ent from the policing at my first police department. There was some-thing more than just arresting the suspects; I had to get more involved in the community. Without gaining the trust of the community, you were not going to know all the issues they were facing, and they were not going to tell you about them due to their distrust of the police.

The gang problem around Lamar University while I was there was mostly the Rollin 60s Crips. They had a house they always partied at just two blocks from the campus, which we paid close attention to. We would drive by the house, and several of us would get together and walk the street in front of the house. If someone left this house and I saw a traffic violation, I would stop them and write them a ticket. One of those times people were at the house having a party. One man stumbled away from the house and into a parking lot of Lamar University. He was obviously intoxicated on something, and we suspected that it was PCP. I was training another guy at the time, and as we jumped out of the patrol vehicle to confront the intoxicated man, he began yelling and screaming at us. He balled up his fists and acted like he was about to rush us and fight. I pepper-sprayed him, and at the same time the guy I was training tased him. The man started crying for his mother. That was a surreal moment—the tough guy transformed into a child right in front of us.

It was a reminder that people we deal with aren't just threats or cases. They are broken in ways you don't always see until the moment cracks them open.

We were able to move them out of the area and all of a sudden, a new group, who called themselves the South Park Bloods, were everywhere. We turned our attention to the houses they were using for their gang activity, as some of the community would give us tips about the problem areas.

One tip led me to a self-serve car wash near the campus. We knew they had been using the area to traffic narcotics, so I pulled into the nearly empty parking lot of the car wash and just parked there, making a visible presence in the area. I figured it would at least stop the drug trafficking as long as I was there, and they would resume as soon as I left. A drug-free hour is better than nothing. I would get out and walk the parking lot of the car wash and look for anything someone might have hidden around the car wash. I wasn't there to make an arrest. It was to remind people that someone was paying attention.

While walking the parking lot one day, I was approached by a man I knew to be a member of the Bloods. He began yelling at me and telling me how much I was a problem for the community and how he owned this corner. I looked at him and, in a calm, clear, and direct manner, told him I owned the neighborhood. He scoffed at me and stepped into the street to cross it. He was jaywalking, a violation of the law, so I promptly arrested him for the offense.

I worked a lot with the community and at one point, people from the community were calling Lamar PD instead of Beaumont PD because the response time was better. It ended up being during the holiday block parties that I would walk the blocks and talk to the families who were celebrating. I even was told at several of the parties to grab a plate and make a meal for myself; it meant a lot to me to be invited into these parties. When I first arrived at the University, the community, made up of mostly African Americans, kept to themselves and did not want anything to do with any of the police. When they witnessed a crime, they just would not say anything about it to us. Now I was being invited over and offered food. It was a stark contrast to the area I first came to when hired.

Soon, I was "voluntold" (volunteered and told that I was going to do something) that I was going to a mental health peace officer school hosted by Houston Police Department, along with another officer. This was a week-long school in Houston to educate on mental health and law enforcement. We were told that the department was not going to provide a room for us or per diem, and we were going to have to drive to class and home from class every day. Most classes are done at the regional police academy or at an agency where the drive wasn't more than thirty minutes or so, but Houston was over ninety miles away, with plenty of traffic. This decision was making us arrive at work at 5:30 a.m. and not return before 8 p.m. all week.

Little did I know that the lessons I had learned at my first police department, combined with the lessons and training I received at Lamar, would launch my career in an unexpected way.

CHAPTER NINETEEN

THE RIVER TRIP

IN THE SUMMER OF THE FIRST YEAR THAT I WORKED AT Lamar PD, I went to Dallas to spend the weekend with my family. I did not know when I began this trip that I would be reminded of a valuable lesson that I knew but let my guard down about. The lesson was that things go from good to horrible in an instant, and we are not in control of when that is going to happen, but we need to prepare for it. My mother, sister, her boyfriend, and my nephew all decided to go to the Brazos River and float down it on rafts. It's a pretty common thing in Texas to float the rivers, and there are several rivers that people float. It's almost always a drunk fest though, and just about everyone drinks alcohol while floating down the river. It's also pretty common that people link up with other groups while floating and hang out and exchange different drinks that were brought to the river just for an all-around fun time. As the hours passed, the drinking caught up with people, and the energy on the river began to change.

We were nearing the end of this float when we observed one of the groups, which we had talked to on the float, start having a commotion on the river. One guy was confronting another guy and telling him to go away. The other guy got in his face and the first guy pushed the other guy, which caused him to fall under the water. When he stood up, he had a large lime-green-handle diving knife in his hand. I did not want my family to be involved in this situation so I told them to get as far away as they could from it. I could not allow someone else to get stabbed and not do anything myself to try and prevent it. So I made my way over to the group.

Everyone circled around the man with the knife. One of the females started talking to the man, and he started dropping his guard. I saw my opportunity to intervene and attempt to stop his aggressive actions. While he was looking at the female who was talking to him, I jumped on the hand with the knife, grabbed it, and held on for dear life. One of the other guys then hit this guy in the face. While the guy was dizzy from being hit in the face, I pried the knife from his fingers and took the knife. I then took the knife over to my family and hid it in an ice chest so no one else would have access to it. This calmed the situation and in less than fifteen minutes, the man who had the knife had passed out drunk in a tube. I floated the rest of the way tense, wondering if I was going to have to break up another fight and knowing there were going to be questions to answer when we arrived at the river's end.

I wasn't on duty and hadn't planned on being anything more than a guy floating the river with his family, but some situations don't care whether you're working or not. Once you step into them, you don't get to pretend they didn't happen. When we made it to the exit on the river, the local Sheriff's Office was waiting for us. I explained that I was a police officer and gave them the knife. Later that week, I received a phone call from a detective at the Sheriff's Office who said he needed a statement from me about the events and that they were investigating the man for an aggravated assault. I wrote them a statement and sent it to them and never heard anything else about it.

The lesson learned was no matter where you are and who you are with, at any time you could be confronted with crime and have to act. In the middle of a river, I was not prepared to act, but had to act anyway. I needed to make sure I was always prepared to act at a moment's notice.

CHAPTER TWENTY

HOW MANY ASSISTANT CHIEFS

THE SECOND ASSISTANT CHIEF OF POLICE WHEN I WAS there at Lamar PD was a good man; the department had three assistant chiefs of police in the three years I worked for them. They all had their strengths and weaknesses, but the second assistant one was my favorite, though several other police officers did not like him. At the end of his tenure at Lamar PD, I think he thought I was not a fan of his, which was not true. The policy he implemented that probably got the most scrutiny was the "wait for backup" policy. He did not want officers responding alone to any incident that presented a possible use of force issue and required two officers to respond. The rub, I believe, was the fact that he required you to wait to respond until another officer was there with you, which took up some valuable time to stop the aggression.

This assistant chief of police showed up several times on calls I worked out in the neighborhood, though, and was always supportive on the calls I went on. I was also made corporal during this time and was assigned to the night shift because the previous corporal left to go to a city police department.

During this time, I also got struck by a DWI driver, who rear-ended me while I was stopped at a red light, causing me to pull some muscles in my back. Needless to say, the DWI driver went to jail; there was also a mandatory blood draw that happened on this driver, which showed his blood alcohol content level at 0.2 when the legal limit was 0.08. The next year, there would be a U.S. Supreme Court ruling that effectively made mandatory blood draws illegal under the fourth amendment. This caused the District Attorney to plead this case down to reckless driving instead of Intoxicated Assault with a Motor Vehicle.

A couple weeks after being hit by the drunk driver, we had the U.S. Marshals and a Texas Ranger show up at the police department. They were searching for a man who had committed an armed robbery in Killeen, Texas, and, during the armed robbery, had shot and killed the clerk of the convenience store he robbed. They had been tracking his location using his cell phone, and it showed he was in the dorms of the University. So, they wanted us to go to the dorm and see if he was there. He was not a student at the University, but his girlfriend was a student and lived in a dorm room.

We had several officers working that night, so we set out to serve the capital murder warrant. We surrounded the building and knew exactly what dorm he was in on the second floor of the door. I stationed myself in the courtyard of the dorms in case he decided to flee through one of the windows. I don't know what this guy was thinking, but when officers got to the second floor, they heard loud music coming from the dorm. They decided to treat it as a loud noise complaint, which happened almost every day in the dorms. When the officers knocked on the door, the wanted suspect answered the door in nothing but a towel. As soon as he saw it was the police, he took off running down the hall of the dormitory. The towel he was wearing did not stay on him, so there he was streaking through the dorm.

When I heard the officers on the radio advise he was running, I started running through the courtyard in the direction he was heading so I could cut him off at the stairs. One of the officers was fast enough to catch up to him and tackled him to the ground. The officer who tackled him had his arms locked around him, and he landed on top of him, causing severe concrete burns across the whole back of his hand. At about the same time, a female officer's foot went between the guy's leg. I'm not sure if it was the female officer's foot making contact with his nether regions or the officer's weight who landed on top of him, but this caused the suspect to lose his bowels all over the female officer's shoe. He then was handcuffed and taken back to the apartment.

The scene settled, but the tension didn't. Even with him in custody, there was a sense that this wasn't finished yet, that the night still had more to take.

The Texas Ranger and the Marshals then came to the dorm room. The guy became really aggressive, even though he was handcuffed, and got in my face. He was yelling at me to kill him to where I thought he was going to assault me and attempt to escape. I unholstered my taser and took the cartridge off. I then tased him; that took all the energy out of him, and he complied from then on.

The taser ended the threat, but it didn't erase the moment. What stays with you is how everything shifts quickly from control to chaos and back again. Those moments stay with you whether anyone notices or not.

Unfortunately, running through the courtyard of the dorms aggravated my injury from getting hit by the DWI suspect. The second assistant chief did not talk to me much during this time, which seemed unusual given the incident. I would have thought he would have checked on me after getting hit by the drunk driver and being on leave for a week. I think he was frustrated with some of the officers, and I was being lumped into his resentment.

When the assistant chief announced that he was leaving Lamar PD to become a chief at a small private university in Houston, they hired another guy from Rio Grande Valley University to become the third assistant chief; that man wanted to bring in one of his friends. I was caught off-guard that he was leaving. He had been a great assistant chief. I had no idea about his replacement and what to expect from him. At the same time, I had applied for an open sergeant's position. However, they changed the hiring criteria for the sergeant position to include preference given to someone with Special Weapons and Tactics (SWAT) training. This move helped solidify that I would not make sergeant, but the friend of the incoming assistant chief would become sergeant without ever working a day on patrol at Lamar PD.

That was the moment it clicked. The process wasn't built to reward the work I'd put in. They didn't tell me I wasn't good enough. They just moved the goalpost until I couldn't reach it. I could live with losing a fair competition, but I was annoyed with how rigged the whole thing was.

The second assistant chief also made sure during the promotional interview to point out all my flaws and none of my strengths to everyone. I think he did this to sabotage my chances because several of the officers I hung around with did not like him and talked badly about him. Since I was around them, he thought I had the same opinion as they did. To top it off, I would have to train the new sergeant as part of his field training. I did not blame the new sergeant for getting sergeant over me and trained him the same way I trained everyone else, but I started having growing resentment for Lamar PD.

I kept doing the job the right way, because that's who I am. I trained him thoroughly, backed him publicly, and never let my frustration bleed into the work, but resentment grows quietly. I knew my feelings for the department were changing even if I didn't want to admit it yet.

It was compounded when in training the new sergeant, it was clear he was not ready to be a sergeant. When the new assistant chief took over, his philosophy was his way or the highway. Anyone who attempted to provide a different viewpoint was immediately stopped, as he made it clear that he was in charge, and it was going to be his only way. That's when I started looking for other law enforcement opportunities in the area.

It wasn't a single bad day that pushed me to start looking at other departments; it was the slow realization that the environment was changing in ways I couldn't fix. I had always believed that effort, professionalism, and patience would eventually be enough, but leadership hardened and voices were shut down. I started to understand that staying would mean accepting a version of the job that didn't align with who I was becoming. I wasn't running from work; I was trying to find somewhere I belonged.

CHAPTER TWENTY ONE

HARDIN COUNTY SHERIFF'S OFFICE

I FELT MY TIME WAS COMING TO A CLOSE AT LAMAR University PD, and thankfully through contacts I had made in the area and a ride-along I had done with a deputy at the Hardin County Sheriff's Office, I decided to further my career and apply. One of the things I looked at before applying was the turnover at the sheriff's office. To my surprise, it seemed like most of the people had been long-term deputies for the department; that brought so much relief because I wanted to find somewhere I could retire, rather than keep changing agencies.

The sheriff personally called me and set up an interview in March/April of 2014. The interview seemed to go extremely well, as the sheriff said my name came to him as highly recommended from a friend of his who worked with him at Texas DPS, and he had recommended me for the job. I was hired at the same time at Lamar as the sheriff's friend, who had retired as a captain with Texas DPS. Soon after, I received a phone call back from the sheriff himself, who told me he wanted to hire me but had picked someone else for the opening. He asked me if he could keep my contact information and call me back the next time they had an opening. I was disappointed but agreed to this.

In September of 2014, the sheriff called me back and asked if I was still interested in employment with the Hardin County Sheriff's Office. I was still interested and started at the end of that month. I told him I was still interested in the job, but the only problem I had was that in a month I had scheduled a vacation to Mexico. The sheriff said that was okay, and he would hire me anyway. Later that day, I received a phone call from the chief deputy to set up a time to get fitted for uniforms.

The sheriff's office had me go through a modified field training program. They worked a four-on, four-off, twelve-hour schedule, and every two weeks, you rotated from days to nights and vice versa. During my FTO time at the sheriff's office, I received phone calls from officers at Lamar PD asking me how certain calls should be handled. They did not trust the leadership they were under to make the right calls and were looking for advice on how to properly handle situations. The FTO I was with at the sheriff's office also took notice of this, since most of the calls were coming in while I was working.

It wasn't a sense of pride. I had already left Lamar, yet people there still trusted me more than the leadership they were answering to every day. I didn't feel validated so much as unsettled, as it forced me to confront a hard truth. Walking away from a place doesn't mean you stop carrying responsibility for the people still inside it.

I went to several stabbings while on FTO, and one of my FTOs said he had seen more blood while FTOing me than he had seen in the previous year. One of those incidents was a golf cart accident where they had been driving the vehicle too fast. When the vehicle rolled, the driver's arm was almost severed from the top of the golf cart landing on her arm. My FTO and I were able to apply a tourniquet to her arm and save her life. After we applied the tourniquet, we were told by a trooper that Texas DPS was not going to work the accident since it happened on a private road, not a public road. My FTO told me I needed to start taking statements and pictures. I started doing one thing, and he got irritated with me that I was not doing the other thing at the same time. I was frustrated; how was I supposed to do two things at once while he watched me?

I felt exposed. The scene was chaotic: a woman was bleeding, and I knew I was being evaluated in real time. Every decision felt heavier because it wasn't just about doing the job. It was about proving I belonged there.

It made more sense as I looked back at the situation now. I was doing things out of order, as he said statements and pictures, and that was the order I was doing things in. However, I needed pictures first because the victim was about to be taken by EMS to the hospital, and I could get the statements at any time after that.

I was only on field training for two months at the County until they thought I was ready to patrol by myself. I was released from training in time to work Thanksgiving. Campus police departments are looked at as quasi-police departments. You have police powers but you just don't see the crimes that you see working for a city or county agency. The achievement I felt being released from FTO in two months solidified that I wasn't just a quasi-police officer, but I had what it took to do real police work.

What surprised me was the relief. I felt steady again, like I had found my footing in a place that expected more from me and trusted me to meet it. I came to find out the sheriff's office did a lot more than I had ever done before. For one thing, working for Hardin County, you are responsible to work any and every misdemeanor case you get all the way to completion. The detectives at the Hardin County Sheriff's Office only worked felony offenses.

This was some invaluable experience and some things that you did not get at most agencies. Now the felony offenses allow you to work them as far as you could work them. If you thought you could solve a felony without the help or with minor help from the detectives, you were encouraged to do so. I dove into the challenge. When I thought I could work a case, I worked it. I learned how to get subpoenas for cell phones and bank records.

At one point, I worked a runaway juvenile case from start to finish, which ended up evolving into a sexual assault of a child. The only thing the detective had to do was go pick up the Sexual Assault Nurse Exam from the hospital for me. I submitted blood to a lab for DNA evidence and was able to tie someone to a burglary. I would have never been able to do any of those things as a police officer at the campus police departments.

While on patrol on day shift, another deputy and I were dispatched to a disturbance with a woman who was attempting to kill herself. When we arrived, we were greeted by an older gentleman who had on a button-down shirt, only the buttons were not buttoned except for a couple of bottom buttons. His shirt was in disarray, and there was some blood on his shirt. We asked him what had happened, and he told us his daughter was attempting to cut herself with a knife. He was trying to stop her when she attacked him for attempting to stop her.

The man was not angry with his daughter; he was afraid of what she might have done. These are the moments that matter. A single bad decision, a second too slow, and the outcome would shift from intervention to tragedy, leaving a father to live the rest of his life replaying what he should have done differently.

This brought me back to thinking about the woman who bit me and how in that moment you never knew what was about to happen. We asked where she was now, and we were shown a bedroom door. He did not know if she had gone into the bedroom with the knife, just that she had not come out of the bedroom.

I knocked on the bedroom door and announced who we were. I did not hear anything come from the bedroom before or after I knocked. I was afraid that the woman had cut herself and was possibly bleeding out and needed immediate intervention to stop her death. I needed to get into that room to help her; coupled with the fact that she had already assaulted her father and knew the sheriff's office was there, this increased the odds that she would attempt to kill herself. I attempted to open the door, but it was locked. Like most bedroom doors, it was a lock that was just child protection, and all you had to do was turn the lock with your thumb and it allowed you entry into the bedroom.

Opening that door meant committing to whatever was on the other side, whether it was a life to save or a threat to stop. There was no way to ease into it, no option to wait it out. Once we went in, there was no pulling back.

I paused for a moment and looked at the other deputy. He nodded his head at me. I turned the lock, and the door was unlocked. I made sure the other deputy knew the door was unlocked, and we were about to go in. Once he nodded his head in agreement, I opened the door. This door opened into the bedroom, and there was a wall just on the other side of the entrance to the bedroom, making the door enter into a hallway between the bedroom and a bathroom.

When we entered, we immediately heard movement from the left side of the hallway where the door was. I focused my attention toward the sounds; that's when I saw a woman running at me with a knife held straight out in front of her. In one instant, my heart started to race, and my mind started to think about all the possibilities of what could go wrong. It felt like time was almost standing still. I could hear the slow march of feet pounding the ground as she ran toward me. The only thing between her and I was this flimsy door, and I had no time to think about what to do next. All I knew was I did not want to get stabbed.

There was no plan forming in my head, no checklist of options. The pressure, timing, and distance collapsed all at once. I could feel how close she was and how fast she was moving. There was little space between action and consequences, and this was not about tactics or courage. It was about reacting.

In police training, they teach you the "twenty-one foot rule." The rule is if someone is within twenty-one feet of you with a knife, they can stab you before you can pull your gun and engage the suspect. We were within five feet, and I had to do something. My only thought was to grab her outstretched hand holding the knife and push it away from me. So that's what I did. I grabbed hold of her wrist with both hands and pushed it toward my right side. At the same time, I took my left forearm and pushed her as hard as I could into the wall opposite of the door. Her whole body slammed into the wall, causing her to immediately drop the knife. I then handcuffed her.

Dispatch had already called for EMS. When EMS arrived, they began looking her over. She was yelling, upset, and was cussing at me for ramming her into the wall. She said I did not need to do that to her, but she was lucky that was all I did to her. I was justified in killing her, and all she got was rammed into the wall. She continued to rant and rave about it so EMS gave her some ketamine to help her calm down and then transported her to a local hospital in Beaumont. Her father did not want to charge her for assaulting him, and I did not file any charge on her for attempting to stab me. I was just relieved I did not have to kill her.

Knowing how close she had come to death, and how permanent the other outcome would have been, left me quiet. I didn't feel victorious; I felt spared. I never got any follow-up about it, and I hope she was able to receive the help she needed at the hospital.

Nothing was ever said about the use of force I had used here. It was a stark contrast to the time I was actually bitten and got in trouble; both times, I had justifiable use of force. The first department wanted to tear me down due to the use of force. The sheriff's office seemed like they were just glad I was not hurt in the situation.

The contrast was remarkable. One department treated use of force as something to scrutinize first and understand later. The sheriff's office recognized that force, when justified, didn't require theater or punishment. That response shaped how safe I felt operating inside the organization. I understood how much a particular leadership philosophy can either erode or reinforce an officer's ability to do the job.

CHAPTER TWENTY TWO

INSTRUCTING

RIGHT BEFORE I LEFT LAMAR PD, I STARTED INSTRUCT-ing at the regional police academy. They needed someone to teach a one-day class on drugs, and I taught that class for a few years. Later, Hardin County sent me to a field sobriety instructor school, and I started teaching that course at the academy. I even got sent to an instructor school to teach police pursuit driving.

Teaching the drug course was good, and I was able to get a handle on talking in front of a group of people. The material itself was pretty dry, as it's not much fun teaching people what the penalty is for possession of this drug or that drug. I did try to make the course a little more interesting by bringing in a bunch of training drugs and allowing them to see them. I would also give them some war stories of some of the drug arrests I had made over the years. From there, I would tell them about how you can further your investigation by just asking questions.

I tried to drive home to the class that most good cases don't start with a search; they start with listening. People will often tell you far more than they intend to if you give them space to talk. Silence makes people uncomfortable, and uncomfortable people start talking. Teaching cadets to slow down, pay attention, and trust their instincts was more important to me than other lessons.

One of my favorite stories to share is to separate the driver and passenger and ask where they are coming from and where they are going. If they give an answer that doesn't match or that doesn't make sense, something is going on. The most common of excuses that just doesn't make sense is we were coming from Point A and going to Point B, but the location they were in was nowhere between the two points. That was a clue that I needed to look further into the situation.

Teaching DWIs was always fun. As mentioned above, I was hit by a DWI at Lamar so it is also something I am passionate about. It was a three-day class, and on the second day you got to bring in people and give them alcohol at a controlled level. The alcohol was provided by Mothers Against Drunk Driving (MADD). Of course, we checked and made sure people were of age and had a sober ride home before we got them drunk. Once they were drunk, we had the cadets come in and perform the field sobriety tests on them. It took two hours to get someone drunk using the matrix that was provided to control the amount of alcohol they got. It is all a mathematical equation based on their weight that tells us how much alcohol they can consume.

People never expect how little alcohol it actually takes to change someone, as people who would swear they can drink a lot were already missing steps, losing balance, or forgetting simple instructions. Others looked drunk long before they believed they were. It drove home a truth that statistics alone can't teach: impairment doesn't announce itself, and confidence is often the first thing alcohol lies about.

It would get pretty comedic nearing the end of the second hour. The drunk people were dancing and singing and having a good time. During the exercise, we gave them portable breath tests at certain intervals so we knew what their levels actually were. In addition, there was normally a person we planted in the group that had not been drinking. At the end, we asked them if they would arrest or not arrest each person based on the results they observed of the field sobriety tests. We then revealed to the class how drunk the people actually were. MADD normally always brought in people who had been affected by drunk drivers to tell their stories and point out why DWI enforcement was a critical element of policing.

Instructing driving was a whole other beast. You had to start them off slow, as the track was really tight, and it was pretty hard to drive the car fast without knocking down cones. As they learned the techniques that were taught, you started to open the track more, which always meant faster speeds. The danger also increased as the speed went up. The first day just dragged on and on. The class wanted to go fast, but every time they did, they murdered the cones on the track. They slowed down and started using the techniques they were taught, and things started getting better for them.

Once you get to the second day, things are moving much faster. By the end of the second day, most cadets were doing pretty good. By the end of the class, not only have they learned some new driving techniques that put them in greater control of their vehicles, they also had a lot of fun. Routinely, we were told that driving was the best class in the academy. The vehicles didn't like it, but the students did.

The things I taught in these classes were not just taught because it was a required piece of the academy so you can sit for the state exam. It was personal. Several other officers I know have also been hit. One of the cadets I helped train in both DWI and driving, on August 9, 2020, was hit head on and killed by a drunk driver while she was a passenger in a patrol vehicle. She was only twenty-three years old.

CHAPTER TWENTY THREE

FIRST MURDER

JANUARY 10, 2016, WAS A COLD AND SLEEPY SUNDAY morning in southeast Texas. It was around 38 degrees outside and for southeast Texas, you could say that's freezing cold. I was on patrol, and there was hardly anyone else out and moving around. Just a vehicle here and there. Boredom sometimes sets in, so you have to figure out how to overcome the boredom. On this Sunday morning, I decided to drive up Hwy 92 to the Hardin County line. One of my favorite convenience stores was at the county line, and nothing says country store like a store that offers gasoline, fishing equipment, and guns all in one store.

There is just something about that place. The kind of stop where nothing ever seems urgent. The morning carried the false comfort that nothing unexpected was waiting for me down the road. Because the morning was so sleepy, I had plenty of time to go up there and do what we call "flying the flag." Flying the flag is driving through areas just to let people know the sheriff's office is around; it visually shows people you are in the area and working. After spending 20–30 minutes driving around the northwest area of the county, I proceeded to head back to civilization and toward the city.

I was driving south on Hwy 92 when I noticed a Black male standing on the shoulder of the highway, wearing shorts and a T-shirt. This guy was frantically waving his arms, attempting to get the attention of a truck that was in front of me. That truck hit his brakes and pulled over. We have a thing we call a spidey sense, and mine went off. I might not be exactly able to tell you what's wrong about the event, but it just did not look or feel right.

Experience teaches you to trust discomfort before you can justify it. Sometimes events just whisper to you, and there was something about his movements that just felt out of place for that quiet Sunday morning. I couldn't articulate it yet, but I knew enough not to ignore it. Those moments, the ones that don't make sense right away, are normally the ones that matter most.

One thing I did notice about the truck that stopped to talk to the guy was that it only had a brake light on the top of the cab, and both side rear brake lights were not working. That gave me a reason to talk to the driver of the truck. The only thing was the vehicle braked in front of me, and I did not have the time to stop behind him so I waited just down from where they were. When the truck departed, the driver decided not to pass the area I was stopped at, doing a U-turn instead, and then turning right down a side street. These moves seemed to be evasive maneuvers and again made those hidden senses say that something just was not right there.

Evasive behavior doesn't have to be dramatic to be meaningful. People who have nothing to hide usually take the simplest path forward. A U-turn when there's no reason, a sudden change in direction, small decisions that add friction where none is needed. Those are tells. Individually, they don't amount to much. Together, they form a pattern that you ignore at your own risk.

So I sped up and stopped the vehicle for the brake lights, knowing in the back of my mind that I was going to be looking for other criminal activity beyond his brake lights not working. It took me about a half mile to get the vehicle stopped. When I talked to the driver, he told me that the other guy had been flagging down traffic and told him someone was out to get him. I told him I would go talk to the other guy after I finished with him.

I was in the process of checking the driver's license and looking over his files on my computer when dispatch radioed me. The dispatcher had a slightly heightened tense voice, which always excites police officers when you can tell she has a "good call." She told me she had just received a 911 call from a father about a disturbance at a residence on Hwy 92 near where I was and that the suspect fled on foot toward the highway. She gave the description of the subject as a Black male and was still getting information about the disturbance. I told dispatch that once I finished this stop, I would head toward the disturbance and that I believed I had already seen the suspect on Hwy 92. It seemed like no time when the dispatcher contacted me again via the radio and said the father had gone to the residence to check on his daughter and had found her dead.

I did not even go back to the driver about the brake lights. I opened my door and shouted at the driver that he was free to go. I made a U-turn and headed back toward where the guy was on the side of the highway. While I was driving down the side street to get to the highway, the dispatcher got back on the radio and told me to hurry up and get there because the father was headed to kill the guy for killing his daughter. Mind you, this is Texas and the county is large. There were only three or four of us working, and I knew that getting someone to come help me was going to be a long proposition. I had not a clue where in the county any of the other officers were, and I was about to face off with someone who just killed someone, which, in and of itself, is a dangerous task. Now I had to also deal with the furious father who was looking for blood himself.

The danger wasn't just the man I was after. It was the collusion course forming around him. A suspect desperate enough to flag down strangers. A father raw enough to kill. Me alone in the space between them, trying to keep one more death from happening. There was no backup close, no margin for error, and no option to slow down. Whatever happened next was going to happen fast, and I was already committed to being in the middle of it.

I was relieved when I got to the highway and saw the Black guy by himself walking down the shoulder of the road. I pulled up behind him, turned on my lights, and got out of the vehicle. Adrenaline was still coursing through my veins and all sorts of thoughts about what might happen were running wild in my head as I approached this guy. I calmly walked up to him, ordered him to turn around and face the hood of my vehicle, and put his hands behind him. Much to my surprise, he did just that.

There was no fight, no resistance; he just completely obeyed my orders and was handcuffed. I did a pat-down of him for weapons because to my knowledge at the time, I assumed he had just assaulted someone, maybe even killed someone, even though I really did not know what was going on. This just felt too easy. My relief was short-lived though as the next thing I noticed was a truck sliding in the grass on the right side of my vehicle passed us, and a tall, slender, older man came towering out of the vehicle. He was angry! My heart immediately began pounding again and the whole thing felt surreal.

The man was yelling and screaming, but I could not figure out what he was yelling for, even though I knew what he was saying. I quickly placed the suspect in the rear seat of my patrol vehicle and was glad it was equipped with a cage.

I then walked toward the angry man and asked him what was going on. I will never forget his answer to that question. "That son of a bitch just killed my daughter!" The next question I asked was where did this happen? I don't know if that surprised the guy or what, but it took some of the wind out of his sails, and he exasperatedly said at his house, while he pointed down the road. I looked at him and told him to "take me there." He nodded his head and got back in his vehicle, driving a hundred or so yards ahead as I followed him.

It was a little unnerving: I had a murder suspect secured behind me, and a grieving father leading me forward. Neither one of them was operating on logic anymore. I wasn't chasing a suspect or escorting a witness, I was trying to keep grief from turning into something irreversible. I knew that the next place we stopped would change everything.

While we were headed to the scene of the crime, the suspect asked me what I was doing, then he started getting scared and asked if I was the cousin of the deceased girl who was a police officer. I really did not know what he was talking about at the time. I was floored that he thought I was related to this family at all. Later, I got a message from a Beaumont police officer that I knew who was the cousin of the woman. The world feels so big and disconnected, and then you find people you know are personally affected by the crimes you are responding to.

It narrows the gap between the job and my own world. This crime wasn't distant; it was connected and personal. It stripped away the illusion that policing happens in isolation from the rest of the world.

I watched the father open the door but I could not see inside due to a blanket drying on the clothesline. The father pulled back the blanket to reveal his daughter lying face down in a pool of blood just inside the doorway of the house. The female was clothed in a white terry cloth robe. Right next to the door was a large flatscreen TV sitting upright on the floor. The TV was on, but there was nothing on the screen but red green and blue square patches. In the pool of blood, you could see foot prints and large smear prints, which reminded me of mud and how when it's the right consistency and drying, you get smear prints. I walked over to the body and checked for a pulse and looked for breathing, but I did not feel a pulse or see the rise and fall of the chest. There was now no doubt this was a murder.

The scene now became a crime scene, the shift was immediate and absolute. Everything was going to have to be solid. Any small mistake was going to be scrutinized and more than one life was on the line.

I exited the house and went to my vehicle to wait for help. You don't do this inside the scene because everything you do has the potential to damage, destroy, or alter the crime scene. So I waited at my vehicle for the cavalry to arrive. While waiting for others, the father approached me. He told me to leave the guy here and come back later. WOW! Did he just tell me that? I politely told him I could not do that. With all the things I have to do, from photographs, searching the house, calling the justice of the peace to pronounce a death, calling the detectives, and so on, I now had to guard my vehicle and the suspect in my rear seat so no one killed him. It felt as if time was standing still. No one had come to help me yet and here I was just sitting there, virtually doing nothing that needed to be done.

After what seemed like an eternity, but I am sure it was only fifteen or twenty minutes, the second officer arrived. My stress and anxiety levels dumped upon his arrival. Now I was not shouldering this entire thing alone. As the growing number of officers arrived, the first detective arrived. He walked over to me to get the basic rundown of the events and what I had already done. After hearing the details, he told me he wanted me to put the hands and feet of the suspect in paper bags. I had paper evidence bags, but I did not have any way of affixing them to his hands and feet, and I had never thought about having to do so. The detective offered some electrical tape from his vehicle.

Standing there, I realized how thin the line was between control and catastrophe. The scene was secure on paper, but not in spirit. This is the part of the job that no one prepares you for. Not the action, but the stillness that follows it. When you're responsible for everything and actively doing nothing.

I took the bags and electric tape to my vehicle and opened the rear door. That's when I saw it: he was covered in blood. I missed the obvious in all the chaos. I now had damning evidence, which support-ed the claims I was already working from.

One of the patrol guys, along with one of the detectives, took the suspect out of my car and carried him to the sheriff's office. I remained at the scene and helped the other detectives process the scene. When we were searching through the house, we located a knife in the sink, which was bent. Looking closer at the knife we found, the very tip of the knife was curled backward; this turned out to be the murder weapon. After we finished processing the scene and the body had been placed in a body bag, the victim was transported to the morgue by a local funeral home. I spoke with the major for the detectives and asked to go to the autopsy. He thought that was a good idea and called me the next day, telling me when to be at the morgue for the autopsy.

When I arrived at the morgue, I was met by the major, along with one of the detectives. We all had to wear paper scrubs over our clothes and paper booties on our boots. The detective also brought with him a camera so he could have department photos of the injury (the morgue also takes their own photographs). When we walked into the room where the autopsy was going to be performed, I smelled the strangest odor. Everyone has heard about how bad a decomposing body smells. I figured there would be some of that odor during this autopsy.

I thought I knew what I was about to walk into. In this job, you build a mental checklist for scenes before you ever arrive. Sights, sounds, smells, as a way to prepare yourself. I expected decay, some-thing sour and unmistakable. I braced for it the same way you brace for a bad call. What I didn't understand yet was that violence leaves its own signature and sometimes it's cleaner, and far more unsettling that anything you can imagine ahead of time.

That was not the case, as the room did not smell like a decom-posing body. It smelled like a butcher shop. "WOW" is all that went through my mind. I had expected the totally wrong odor. The doctor performing the autopsy was told I had never been to an autopsy so while he was doing the autopsy, he narrated what he was doing and why he was doing it. He showed me all the stab wounds and was able to determine if they had happened before death or after death. The doctor found over forty stab wounds on her body. It's almost unexplainable the amount of rage and horror all those stab wounds represented. There were several that were defensive in nature in the arms and such. There were several in the top of her head. There also were three in her neck and chest, which any one of the three would have caused death in just a few minutes. I tried to put myself in the suspect's shoes, but I just couldn't do it. What can another person do to you that would release that much rage?

In 2018, the suspect, Joseph Latulas, pleaded guilty to murder and asked for a sentence to be imposed by a jury. I testified at the trial. When I got on the stand, it was eerie. It was storming outside, and the lights in the courtroom were flickering. I was able to answer all the prosecution's questions in about an hour on the stand, and the defense attorney did not ask me any questions, but reserved the right to call me back to the stand later if some questions arose. Once I stepped down off the stand, all I could do was wait for the verdict. The weight of waiting just sat in the pit of your stomach.

In court, there is a standard called "The Rule" where once the judge orders that anyone testifying cannot talk about the case, and since the defense attorney wanted to be able to call me back, I could not hear the testimony of the other witnesses. The trial lasted for three days. The prosecution had me get Latulas's discipline records from while he was in jail and called me back to testify about his conduct in jail. Once both sides rested, the jury then deliberated. It took the jury approximately forty-five minutes to decide Latulas's fate. Before the jury was called back into the courtroom, the sheriff's office received word that the father was going to take matters into his own hand if he did not feel the jury gave him a fair sentence. That statement made it to every deputy on duty placed in the courtroom.

It wasn't a threat we took lightly. Grief doesn't allow you to follow rules, and when it hardens into resolve, it can turn volatile fast. Our presence wasn't about intimidation, or control; it was about prevention. about making sure a man who had already lost everything didn't lose the last piece of himself by doing something he could never undo.

The atmosphere in the courtroom was somber. I was hoping the jury would give the maximum penalty of life in prison. The family had been through enough, and I did not want to have to arrest the father for taking matters into his own hands. I did not blame him for feeling that way, but I still had to uphold the law, and this was our legal system.

This was one of the moments where empathy and duty run parallel but never meet. I could understand how someone might want to take matters into their own hands, but understanding it didn't make it acceptable. The law doesn't bend for grief, and neither could I.

Once the jury was seated back in the courtroom, they were asked to read their sentence. Latulas received life in jail for the murder. Once the sentencing was complete, all the deputies were now shuffled to positions around the courthouse and in the parking lot. We wanted to make sure no harm came to any of the jury members as they exited the court. I was placed at the main door to the courthouse. Just about every jury member who exited the courthouse that day walked up to me and extended their hand to thank me.

Their thanks caught me off guard. I wasn't a deputy managing crowd flow or watching exits; I was a witness to a system that had worked the way it was supposed to. Twelve strangers had carried an unbearable story, weighed it carefully, and returned a decision that couldn't undo the harm, but could stop it from repeating. I felt the rare relief that comes when justice doesn't feel abstract—it feels human.

At this point I had been to several trials, mostly for DWIs, but it was the first time I had ever had the jury come and shake my hand and thank me for the work I had done. As I stood there to protect them and shook their hands, my heart was melting. The defense attorney even approached me. He told me a lot of officers are good at doing police work, and some are good at testifying in court, but rarely do you get both. He told me I did a great job. Out of all the accolades I had ever received, this one meant the most to me.

It all felt surreal. I had seen a suspicious person flagging down a truck. I had made a traffic stop on the truck. I had been told the suspicious person was involved in a domestic disturbance and then escalated into a murder. How did I just end up exactly at the right time and place? How many people just give up when they have just committed this type of brutal murder? I don't have concrete answers to any of these questions and still don't today.

CHAPTER TWENTY FOUR

SHIFT PARTNERS

THE FIRST SHIFT I WAS PLACED ON AT THE SHERIFF'S office became like family. We ate every meal together. If it was time to eat and someone was on a call, everyone else would wait for the others before they went to eat.

We knew each other's families, and my shift partners became my family. I was not married and did not have a steady girlfriend, so it was not uncommon that on our days off, we would meet up and watch the ballgames or other major events together. We bought each other Christmas gifts. We were a family outside our family, and this also extended to some of the judges and clerks.

The judges gave us keys to the outside doors of their office buildings; that way when everything was closed, we had access to buildings in various parts of the county where we could use the restroom and eat if we needed to eat in peace and quiet. Since I did not live in the county, I placed a set of clean clothes in a closet in one of the judge's office buildings.

We even took some trips together. A memorable trip we took was to float the Frio River in the Hill Country of Texas. We rented a large cabin that slept fifteen or twenty people, and all carpooled for the five-hour trip to the Hill Country. We stopped once we were close to the cabin and bought food to cook and all split the cost. We spent three days out there, and it was all fun and games and I think at some point, everyone got pushed into the pool when they least expected it.

One Valentine's Day, one of my partners got a call about a vehicle that was all over the road. It was mid-morning, but there's still a slight possibility that it was a DWI. When my partner got to the store where the vehicle had last been seen, he found out from employees that it was a very elderly man. The elderly man was going to the store to buy his wife a present for Valentine's Day. The store customers had taken the man back home. My partner then went to the store and bought gifts for the man, while some of the customers helped pay. I don't remember now how I got involved with this, but I ended up going to the house with my partner to drop off the gifts. I took a photograph of my partner giving the gifts to the man to give to his wife. I then sent the picture and a brief statement in a text message to the other guys on our shift and their wives. One of the wives decided to put it on social media. All of a sudden, the news media got ahold of the story and wanted to interview us.

I had always looked for this type of camaraderie from the different places I had worked, but it was all coming together at the Hardin County Sheriff's Office. I now understood why people stayed at this agency for their whole career instead of bouncing from one department to another in search of something more.

CHAPTER TWENTY FIVE

RUN OVER BY SON

ONE AFTERNOON, I OVERHEARD THE LUMBERTON FIRE and Emergency Medical Services (EMS) Department get toned out for a lady who was hit by a vehicle and was needing the ambulance. The dispatcher did not pick up on the fact there was something not right about the call, but from the details of the call, I just felt something was off. There was a gut feeling that someone does not just get run over by their son in their front yard. I told dispatch to have an EMS stage and wait for officers before proceeding to the call.

Well, my message was too late, and EMS was already on scene when I arrived. As I rolled up, I saw a truck with mud all down the side from the wheels spinning and throwing mud. The truck was parked against the side of the trailer house. There were mud trails and torn-up grass, which appeared to be where the truck had done donuts in the front yard before hitting the trailer home. In the front yard of the trailer, a man was kneeling down on the ground in the middle of the torn-up yard. Neighbors were pointing to the man and saying he was the suspect.

In moments like that, neighbors want distance from the threat, and families want the violence to stop. My job wasn't to join that momentum; it was to slow it down. Before I could protect anyone else, I had to take control of the person that everyone believed had already crossed the line.

I walked over to him, placed him in handcuffs, patted him down for weapons, and placed him in the rear seat of my patrol vehicle. Because I handcuffed the man, out of an abundance of caution, I Mirandized him before asking him any questions. He said that he lived in the trailer with his mother, sister, and nephew. He said he became upset because he was not allowed to go to a court hearing, which awarded the trailer to his mother. The person who previously owned the trailer did not want his sister living in the trailer, but his mother was allowing it. The man was trying to knock the trailer off its foundation with his truck.

When I spoke with the nephew, he told me his uncle was upset and began doing donuts in the yard while everyone else was in the trailer. When he went outside, his uncle had hit his grandmother with the truck and was inside her vehicle pouring gasoline on the passenger seat. He said he attempted to stop his uncle from destroying his grandmother's car when the uncle picked up the gas can with one hand and had a lighter in the other hand and threatened to set him on fire. The nephew said he picked up a pitchfork and ran at his uncle, which caused him to get away from the car and stop the aggression.

What could easily sound like a wild story was actually a series of desperate, split-second decisions made by people trying to survive someone they loved. The nephew wasn't acting out of violence; he was reacting to imminent danger. Fear becomes practical, and ordinary people do whatever they can to interrupt disaster, even if it means grabbing the nearest thing that looks like a weapon.

When I looked in the grandmother's car, there was an overwhelming smell of gasoline. I had an arson investigator with Lumberton Fire respond to the scene to work the attempted arson investigation. Then I talked to the neighbor who said the guy was driving crazy and doing donuts in the yard. The grandmother came out of the trailer house and attempted to get him to stop. The guy started backing his truck in a ramming motion into the trailer. At one point, the grandmother placed herself between the truck and trailer. The neighbor said the guy looked right at the grandmother and proceeded to ram the trailer again, hitting his mother.

The mother/grandmother was transported to the hospital where she was diagnosed as having broken her leg when she was hit by the vehicle. I charged the man with two counts of aggravated assault with a deadly weapon, one for hitting his mother with the vehicle and one for placing the nephew in fear of serious bodily injury or death by raising the gasoline can and lighter up, threatening to catch him on fire. I also charged him with attempted arson for the vehicle.

The man asked for a trial by judge in this case. Because of his actions in the courtroom, he was actually removed from the courtroom for the trial. I testified in his case, and he was found guilty on one count of aggravated assault with a deadly weapon. The arson charge was deferred to the aggravated assault he was found guilty of and found not guilty for one of the aggravated assaults. He was sentenced to eight years in prison for the crime.

The family loved this man and did not want to see him go to prison. However, it was my duty to protect them and make sure no one else would be hurt. Sometimes you have to make the hard choices that other people don't want to make. The burden of those decisions is great. Arrest and prosecution tear a family apart, but if you don't do it, the next time you are there, you just might be working a murder instead of an assault.

That understanding doesn't make the work easier; it makes it heavier. You carry the looks, the anger, the disappointment, knowing that in someone else's story, you're the villain. The job isn't about being liked or spared from resentment. It's about intervening early, even when it fractures relationships, because waiting feels kinder only until it becomes irreversible. I learned that prevention rarely looks compassionate in the moment, but the alternative leaves a body where a warning once stood.

CHAPTER TWENTY SIX

MICHAEL THE ARCHANGEL

ONE NIGHT, DISPATCH CONTACTED ME ABOUT A PURsuit from Liberty County that was entering Hardin County. They told me that Liberty County had seen this vehicle in a known drug area of their county, and they attempted to make a traffic stop on the vehicle. The vehicle just did not stop and continued heading north into Hardin County.

The vehicle was not "running" from them; it just was not stopping for them. This wasn't something at this point of my career that was too exciting. If the vehicle was not running, it could be anything. My sergeant and I started heading toward the pursuit. The pursuit was heading through an area of the county that is nothing but trees and not many people live in the area. Due to the rural nature of the area and the fact that it's all timberland, there were no street lights, and the canopy of the trees blocked the moonlight.

We located an area where we could hide in the trees and not be seen. Our thought was if we hid in the trees, the suspect would not be able to hit us with his car, thus it would be safer for us to throw spikes in this area. Several police officers have been hurt or killed while throwing spike strips, and we did not want to be the next statistic. The pursuit was the only vehicle on the road at this time of night. There was the suspect's vehicle and several police vehicles following it. When we heard sirens in the distance, we knew they were getting close to us. We told the other officers through dispatch that we were about to spike the vehicle. I can still hear the *cla-clunk* sound the tires made as the vehicle rolled over those spikes, and then the sound of a vehicle rolling on flat tires. We did not just get one tire; we got them all.

The suspect drove about a quarter-mile more and then stopped in the middle of the street. He was promptly taken into custody and given to Liberty County deputies. The danger didn't disappear, but it changed shape. The spikes did what they were supposed to do, and no one got hurt doing it. That mattered more than the adrenaline or the small sense of victory. I'd seen how quickly pursuits could turn fatal, not for the suspects, but for officers standing on dark roads with limited options. This one ended the way they were supposed to: controlled, contained, and without adding another name to a memorial wall.

A couple weeks later, at about 4 a.m., all my partners and I had just sat down to eat breakfast before going home for the day. EMS had been sent to handle a call about someone who needed to go to the hospital. About ten minutes later, my cell phone rang; it was one of the medics who got called on the above call. She said she needed help with the guy and that there was something mentally off with him. I told her we would be there in a few minutes since we were close by at a Waffle House. We left without eating and headed that way.

When we arrived, the vehicle we had spiked a few weeks earlier was sitting in the driveway; it still had the flat tires from the spikes. EMS approached us and told us the male was inside the house in only his tighty-whities. They told me he was talking about having sex with his mother and vividly talking about killing kittens during the day.

We entered the house and spoke with this man's mother. She told us he had been in the military and while in the military, his kidneys or liver stopped cleaning out his system the way it was supposed to. The doctors were trying to figure out what could be done for him and had to keep changing his medications. She said he acted like this every time his medications stopped working. We then went to talk to him. He had gotten dressed in clothes by the time we started to talk to him. He said he was Michael the Archangel, telling us about killing kittens earlier in the day, but there was no evidence that he had actually killed any kittens. His statements were very bizarre, and we feared for his mother's safety.

While talking to him, I told him that he was going to need to go to the hospital so they could check on him. The man yelled at me and said he was not going to the hospital. I calmly told him he was going to the hospital one way or another and that we did not want to hurt him, but get him some help. He stood up quickly and I thought, great, now it's time to fight. He then turned around, and we handcuffed him without issue. I transported him to the hospital, and he was released to the care of the hospital after that.

EMS was grateful that we showed up. It was two female medics, and they did not want to fight or be hurt by this man.

CHAPTER TWENTY SEVEN

NOT GOING BACK

IT WAS A SATURDAY MORNING WHEN WE RECEIVED word that a man was wanted for a blue warrant. A blue warrant is one issued for someone who is out on parole from the Texas Department of Criminal Justice, which operates the state penitentiary system. One of the game wardens lived near where this guy was staying and had seen him go into the location.

The word on the street was this guy had been telling people that he would never go back to the penitentiary. The game warden was keeping an eye on the house and could see if he left. All the patrol guys started to head to the location to attempt to arrest him. Before we got there, the man got into a lifted diesel Dodge Ram, and headed right toward us. When he made the turn onto the highway, one of the deputies was waiting for him.

As soon as he saw the deputy, the pursuit was on. I was just south of them on the same highway headed north to join up with the other deputy. This highway was a two-lane road with a center turning lane, which joined the southbound lane with the northbound lane. The man turned south and now was headed toward me. I made a U-turn and waited on the shoulder for them to make it to me. The other deputy was driving a Ford Explorer and said on the radio that he was having trouble keeping up with the truck.

When they made it to me, the other deputy asked me to take the lead, since his vehicle was barely keeping up with the truck. I was in a Chevy Tahoe, which was a little faster than the Ford Explorer. Traffic was not bad, even though it was about mid-day. When we entered the City of Lumberton, we were doing 120 mph. There was a surge of adrenaline as the vehicle shook under the high speeds. The traffic was not very heavy, but there were still cars that would get in the way, especially at those speeds. You never realize how much rocks and debris are in that center turning lane until you are behind someone going that fast, and he is slinging rocks all over your vehicle.

The city police department shut down the major intersections through the city for us, but because there were two sheriff's office vehicles already in the pursuit, they did not join in. Texas DPS joined in the pursuit just south of the city limits. The trooper's Tahoe was faster than mine and the Explorer, and it did not take long before he was the lead unit in the chase. The highway turned into a limited access highway, those that have entrance and exit ramps.

The sergeant got on the radio and said he believed he just blew the motor in his Tahoe as he was trying to catch up with us. The truck decided to exit the highway without using the exit ramp. The trooper followed him across the grassy median and onto the service road. Both the other deputy and I stayed on the highway. When the truck got to the on ramp for the highway, he entered the highway and continued southbound. We were getting close to the county line at this point, and dispatch had already alerted Beaumont PD to the pursuit.

When we got into Beaumont, the limited access highway became a highway under construction, with two lanes and had concrete walls lining the road. The traffic significantly picked up in this area. About five miles into the City of Beaumont, the truck decided to exit and started driving down the city streets. About a mile later, the truck wrecked out into a fence. When the driver exited the truck, he had a knife in his hand. The trooper aimed right for him, and he began to run. He fell as he was running, and the knife went flying. We jumped out to apprehend him. The smell of burning brake pads was everywhere as we apprehended the man.

The man was taken to the Hardin County Jail and booked for evading arrest in a motor vehicle as well as the blue warrant. He ended up getting time for the pursuit and then sent back to the penitentiary. It turned out the sergeant did not blow his motor, but he ran out of gas, funnily enough.

CHAPTER TWENTY EIGHT

JUST LIKE BONNIE AND CLYDE

IT WAS A COLD NIGHT IN THE MIDDLE OF WINTER, around midnight, when Sour Lake PD got into a pursuit with someone who had just stolen a vehicle. The pursuit was very short-lived because the driver wrecked out. When he wrecked out, he took off running on foot. I arrived after the suspect wrecked out. We attempted to locate him, but due to low light, not knowing exactly where he went, and not having a K9 available to assist with the search, we were not able to locate the suspect. Sour Lake PD already knew who the suspect was and details about the vehicle theft. We all felt like continuing to search for the man was going to be fruitless and since he already knew who it was, all we needed to do was get a warrant for his arrest and he would eventually be found.

About five hours later, Sour Lake PD called out that they were in pursuit of another vehicle. We were shocked at first, as Sour Lake is a small town of under five thousand people. Nothing seemed to ever happen over there, yet there they were in the second pursuit of the night. The vehicle was headed west toward Batson. By the time I was able to get to Sour Lake, they were already ten miles ahead of me. The whole time I was wondering if, by chance, it just might be the same guy from the first pursuit. I made a phone call to the constable in Batson and alerted him to the pursuit that was in his area. I knew he lived in Batson, and he was always ready to help out.

The pattern was forming in my head. Two pursuits in the same night, in the same place where nothing ever really happened, rarely stayed separate for long. I didn't have proof, just the weight of experience. The longer I listened to the radio traffic, the more certain I became that we weren't dealing with coincidence anymore. This was the same chaos continuing down a different stretch of road.

When they got to Batson, the guy made a huge mistake. He turned right instead of left at the only stop sign in the town. Unbeknownst to him, the right turn was a dead end in about half a mile. He ended up driving into the field, which was filled with several pumpjacks that were pulling oil out of the ground.

It was pitch black out in this field, and there were trees everywhere. Sour Lake PD lost sight of the vehicle, but there was only one way in and out of the area. So I stayed in the area waiting for him to leave. About 6:30 a.m., I spotted the truck attempting to leave the field; the sun was starting to come up. He looked right at me, and the pursuit was on again. It was short-lived as he ran the vehicle he had stolen into a pond near the pumpjacks. I continued to look for the guy with no luck. He was left this time in the middle of nowhere in the cold.

That same day, I began getting calls from agencies in west Texas. They knew the suspect very well and were attempting to track him down for multiple vehicle thefts that had occurred from the Lubbock area all the way to southeast Texas. According to the other agencies, the man had told family members he was going to go out like Bonnie and Clyde.

The next day, there was a stolen vehicle in Batson. The stolen vehicle was later found in Baytown, a suburb of Houston, approximately sixty miles from Batson. Near the location where the vehicle was found, there was a stolen Dodge Challenger Hellcat. The next day, the county just south of Hardin County, Jefferson County, went in pursuit of a stolen Dodge Challenger Hellcat. The car was leaving the pursuing deputies in the dust. They found it wrecked out in a very rural area of the county. From there, they attempted to locate the driver but he had disappeared into the woods again. I could not believe it was happening again.

The next morning, in Jefferson County, a farmer was driving on the highway. He looked over and saw one of his trucks, which should have been parked, driving down the highway next to him. He picked up his cell phone and alerted the Jefferson County Sheriff's Office. The deputies got into a pursuit with this stolen truck, and it wrecked out. By this time, the suspect was so cold and hungry from his multi-day, multi-crime spree that he decided to allow the deputies to capture him. At least he would be warm and have food. The man who thought he was a modern-day Clyde and had seemingly escaped the long arm of the law had done so until Mother Nature came calling.

CHAPTER TWENTY NINE

DEPUTY DEATH

IT WAS NOT LONG INTO WORKING AT THE SHERIFF'S OF-
fice before I got pinned as the deputy that was always getting the death
calls. One of my shift partners had his wife make me a T-shirt that said
"Hardin County Death Investigation Unit" on it. Another shift partner got me a few patches from military units that had the grim reaper
on it. It even got the attention of the detectives. One detective, when
it was his week on call, would ask me if I was going to be working
the weekend because if I was, he knew he was probably going to get a
phone call about a death.

I don't know if it was me always being at the right place at the right
time or if the dispatchers just wanted to keep me busy so I did not
keep them busy, or a mixture of both, but it always seemed I was the
one they sent to all the death calls. Granted, most of the death calls
were caused by natural causes. I had worked two separate days on patrol when I had responded to four different death investigations in one
twelve-hour shift. Those days were always hard to get through. Deaths

by natural causes are fairly straightforward, especially when the person is already in hospice care with a known condition that causes death, but you are still meeting with the grief-stricken family. You have to ask them to make hard decisions that they might have not thought about, like which funeral home they wanted to use. You stay at the scene until the funeral home picks up the body. Sometimes it's a silent event; sometimes the families are just grateful someone is there with them. They might offer you coffee and talk about the person. Either way, it's always filled with great sadness.

There are a few different ways death calls typically come into the sheriff's office. The first way is the welfare check, the most dreaded call for anyone. It's normally a friend or family member calling saying they haven't spoken with a person in a week or two and it's not like them to not call or answer their phone. When you get there, it's normally pretty quiet as you don't see any signs of people moving around the residence. There's sometimes an indescribable stench emanating from the place for the smell is directly related to the temperature within. The cooler it is, the less it smells; the warmer it is, the greater the smell. The warmer temperature speeds up the deterioration of the body. The deterioration of the body attracts flies, and sometimes those flies can be seen on the windows of the residence as you walk up to it.

No amount of training prepares you for the first time you actually see it. You can understand decomposition academically, know the science behind it, explain it calmly to someone else, but when you're standing there taking in a dead body with all your senses, your senses sharpen and recoil all at the same time. You learn quickly that death leaves signatures long before you ever find the body, and once you've recognized those signs, you never walk up to a quiet house the same way again.

I can still vividly picture a lady that I found this way; her mouth was open, and hundreds of flies were flying out of her mouth. These calls are complex. You don't have a reason for death, and you have to look for it. Was it natural, a homicide, or a suicide? That's why you are there; to gather facts to help determine the cause of death.

The next way, and probably the most common, is where a family member wakes up in the morning and finds their loved one has passed away and calls 911 for medical assistance. This was the same way my father was found. These are fairly simple, and there typically is not much decomposition yet in the body so the smell is not bad, and the flies haven't shown up yet. Many times, you find these people asleep, and it's fairly peaceful. Sometimes there are known medical issues and they were expected to die, so they returned home to live out their days at home and not in a hospital.

The other way we get notified about deaths are through 911 calls, which are active scenes. A wreck, a disturbance, or some other event has led to someone's death or immediate need for medical attention.

Another thing you get to do as a police officer is death notifications. Sometimes it comes from a hospital, sometimes from another police department, and other times from a county morgue. They almost always ask you to go to a residence in the county and attempt to contact a family member. If you are able to get in touch with the family member, have them call the office that sent you out there. These can come at any time during the day, but they seem to mostly happen during the night.

Imagine it is 3 a.m. You are going to a house you probably have never been to. Most people are asleep so you are having to wake them just to give them the hard news that one of their loved ones has died. It's not fun. There is no glamorous way to do it, and the reaction you get can be very difficult.

At this point in my career, I have gotten numb to death; it is a fact of life. We are all going to die, and nothing we do can stop it from happening. I have seen it at all stages of life, and it always leaves me with a feeling that there just must be more to life than this.

CHAPTER THIRTY

SHOOTING DEATH IN LUMBERTON

THE 911 CALL CAME IN, AND I GOT DISPATCHED TO A shooting. All the information that we had was the caller said her son had just shot her boyfriend. So all the deputies in the county were heading that way, with lights and sirens at speeds well over the speed limit. EMS would stage and wait for law enforcement to clear the scene before they would help whoever was shot, so time was of the essence to make the scene safe and get medical help for the victim.

The caller's house was located just outside the City of Lumberton, so a couple Lumberton police officers also started that way, getting there a minute or so before I got there. They had a man handcuffed and were walking him out of the backyard. They brought him to me, and I double-checked to make sure he did not have any weapons on him. From there, I placed him in the rear seat of my car. The car had a cage in it, which made it a secure area that he would not be able to get out of. We found a man slumped over on the floor in the living room of the house near the front door. We cleared the rest of the house and had EMS come check on the man. EMS got there and started doing their thing in an attempt to save the man's life. I was outside getting the paperwork and things needed to take statements from the other people who were there.

The suspect began yelling and screaming in the patrol car. He was also banging his head against the side window of my car. He then laid down in the back seat and picked his feet up and started kicking the side window of my vehicle. I yanked open the rear door of the vehicle and pulled him out of the back seat. My sergeant and I made the suspect sit on the ground. He kept trying to kick at us and yell and scream, so I got a set of leg cuffs out of the back of my vehicle and placed them on his ankles. They also have about a one-foot chain on them, allowing for someone to walk but making running virtually impossible.

He continued to try to kick at us. I stood on the chain of the leg cuffs so it would limit his movements; that really made him mad. He started yelling and screaming and telling me to get off the chain on his legs. I told him I was not going to get off the cuffs until he calmed down. The man began snarling and drooling. He wrenched his face and, in almost a demonic tone, told me he just killed a man and he could kill me, too. An EMS worker saw him acting this way, and my sergeant asked him if there was anything they could do to help. EMS went to the ambulance and came back with a syringe full of some medication, which they gave to him. Within ten minutes, the guy was asleep. He was then loaded into the ambulance, and they monitored him. I ended up having to ride in the ambulance with them to the hospital.

I wasn't thinking about charges or reports; I was thinking about whether or not he would wake up again angry, violent, or worse. This was no longer a law enforcement problem; it was a human one, unfolding in a confined space with no room for mistakes.

On the way to the hospital, he began to wake up and started acting the same way. The EMS workers gave him another shot, and he went back to sleep.

We were in the hospital for about an hour when he started to wake up again. He immediately started to yell and scream at the hospital so the doctor ordered some antipsychotic medication for him; that medication made him go to sleep for around five hours. During the time he was asleep, a defense attorney showed up at the hospital. This is strange because it was now around midnight, and normally you never see attorneys at that time of night. The attorney said he had been assigned the suspect's case in another criminal matter and that they had gone to court that morning, and he had gotten the suspect released from jail.

The defense attorney and I were just sitting in the hospital room, waiting for the suspect to wake up. We struck up a conversation because there was nothing else to do while we waited. Although I can't remember what we talked about now, it was a good conversation. An hour or so later, a Texas Ranger showed up and said he was assisting in the investigation. When the suspect finally woke up, he was not yelling and screaming anymore, and the doctors continued to monitor his condition. Someone from my department came and took over for me at the hospital. I was able to go home and sleep while the detectives and Texas Ranger finished the investigation.

When I came into work the next shift, I found out that the suspect was interviewed at the sheriff's office and then released. They were going to send the case to the grand jury. It came out in the investigation that the suspect and the victim were in a backyard pool, and both had been drinking. An argument ensued, and the victim went and got a gun and confronted the suspect. The suspect was able to wrestle the gun away from the victim and shot him with his own gun as the victim still was attacking the suspect. The grand jury did not charge the suspect, and he faced no charges for the incident. It was ruled that it was self-defense, since the boyfriend was the one who produced the gun and aimed it at the suspect first.

Someone was still dead, someone else had to live with that reality, and I was left carrying another scene in my head. These were the kinds of calls that didn't stay neatly in a box, and over time, they began to stack on top of each other, whether I wanted them to or not.

By this point in my career, these calls weren't just staying on the job anymore. They were following me home, sitting quietly in the back of my mind, waiting for the next one to join them. I was still doing the work, still showing up steady and professional, but I was carrying more than I realized. Each scene carried weight, not enough to break me outright, but enough to change how I moved through the job. I was becoming more guarded, more cautious, and more aware of how quickly a situation could turn irreversible. I didn't have the language for it then, but looking back, this is the point where the job stopped being something I did and it became something I carried.

CHAPTER THIRTY ONE

DEATH IN CUSTODY

ONE EARLY MORNING, AT 2:15 A.M., WHILE I WAS WORK-ing the night shift, I was dispatched to the far northwest corner of the county. To get there, you actually have to leave Hardin County and enter Liberty County, then take another road back into Hardin County. The caller told 911 dispatchers that her son was going crazy and tearing up the house. It was a good forty-five-minute drive to this address while having my emergency lights and sirens on. A few minutes later, another caller called 911 and said she had just received a code word from her sister, which they had devised so she could alert her sister to whether her son was trying to kill her or not. Upon hearing this, I asked the dispatcher to get an ambulance to start toward the scene because I knew the ambulance was going to be farther away than I was and due to the nature of the call, someone would likely be injured when I arrived. I had a funny feeling that this call was going to be someone extraordinary. I did not know what had happened or what would happen, but all the signs were there that this wasn't a normal call.

Calls rarely come with guarantees, only indicators. The coded language, the request for help before it was too late, the quiet urgency. I didn't know what I was driving into, but I knew enough to treat it as something already in motion, something that wouldn't wait for me to get there.

It was pitch black in the middle of the forest in this part of the county. The emergency lights and sirens were bouncing off all the trees, making for a dizzying drive. I had also reached out to a constable in the area who knew the people in the area to see if he had any other information about this family. The constable told me the man was an enforcer for a Texas prison gang and a bad dude. Another deputy was dispatched with me, and we arrived at about the same time.

There was a group of people standing in the road. We parked, got out, and talked to them, one of which was the first caller. She said her son came over and went berserk. When I asked where he was now, I was told he was still in the house and that they could hear him inside the house every once in a while. While we were talking to the family, the Constable showed up to assist us. We quietly made our way up to the house. The house was tiny, with one room serving as the kitchen, bedroom, and living area. The only area with a door was a bathroom. I peered into the window of the house and noticed that a refrigerator and a chest of dresser drawers had been pulled down in front of the house. I could see into the whole house, but there was a problem. We could hear someone on the inside, but we couldn't see anyone. He must be hiding in one of the corners of the house nearest to us, and he had barricaded the door with the refrigerator and chest of drawers.

I went back to the resident and got their permission to enter the house. We approached very cautiously. The house was slightly elevated and had four or five steps leading to the door. When I opened the door, it only opened ten inches or so, and then the refrigerator and chest of drawers blocked the door from opening more. It was a good thing, though, that no one charged at us when the door opened. I was able to look in the corners where I thought the suspect could be hiding. I did not see anyone, which was perplexing. We had heard him in the house making a grunting noise. I had looked almost everywhere except the bathroom, so that's where he had to be.

I started pushing on the door, trying to push the refrigerator and chest of drawers enough to give me room to enter. It moved some, but not near enough for me to get in. I pushed on the door again, and that's when I heard a grunt again. I realized the grunting sounds were coming from under the refrigerator. I looked down, and there he was underneath them.

We really had to get inside now so all three of us started to push on the door. The door opened enough that the constable was able to climb over the stuff and enter the house. I gave the constable a pair of my handcuffs, and he cuffed the suspect. He then got the refrigerator and chest of drawers off of the guy so we all could enter. I attempted to wake the guy, but he was unconscious and was not going to wake up. He was approximately 450 lbs., shirtless, and covered in prison gang tattoos. Those prison tattoos denote a hatred of his fellow man and membership in white supremacy gangs, but here we were trying to do everything we could to save him. He was a big guy and must have been under those things for an hour or so before we were able to get it off of him.

Lying there, pinned beneath the weight, he looked less like a threat and more like a problem no one had solved in time. The tattoos told one story, violence, loyalty to something brutal, but the body told another. Unconscious. Helpless. Dependent on the same system he had likely spent years resisting. It struck me how often law enforcement meets people at the exact moment when every bad decision had already been made, and all that was left was damage control. Whatever he had done before that night no longer mattered. In that moment, he wasn't an enforcer or a gang member. He was a human being whose life now depended entirely on how fast the rest of the system could work.

I asked dispatch to go ahead and have the medics come up to the scene instead of staging. Common practice is that the medics wait on law enforcement to secure the scene prior to them getting on scene for the safety of everyone involved. The problem was the medics had not arrived yet. We continued to wait for the medics to arrive, and as we waited, we noticed a syringe lying on the floor. In this area, methamphetamine was a huge problem. After about fifteen minutes, we asked dispatch to check on the status of the ambulance. We were told they were almost on scene.

In the meantime, the man's breathing changed. Instead of the regular breaths, his breaths became short and raspy and had a gurgling sound associated with it. I made sure the man was on his side as much as possible, which was an issue because he kept rolling over. I asked dispatch to have them step it up (police jargon for getting here faster). The ambulance still took an additional thirty minutes or so to get there. When the ambulance finally arrived, I exited the house and explained to them what was going on. I also told them I believed it was a possible methamphetamine overdose. They came to the house and started to assess the situation.

Watching them work, I felt the tension shift from uncertainty to urgency. This was no longer a containment problem; it was a race against time that had been running since before we arrived. Every minute that passed felt heavier than the last. His breathing wasn't just labored; it was wrong, and I knew enough to recognize when a body started slipping past the point of no return. I remembered thinking how thin the margin had become, how quickly a call that begins as chaos can turn into something irreversible when help is too far out and options are running out.

The biggest issue was getting the overweight man up and out of the house. EMS devised a plan to use a sheet off the bed to help move him. I took all five of us to move him (two medics and three cops). Once we got him to the steps of the door, we had to set him down. We then positioned the stretcher to place him on the stretcher for transport to the hospital; the man was still handcuffed during this. Once he was on the stretcher, he was seatbelted to the stretcher. One of the medics lifted the stretcher up, fully extending it to the top level so he could push him to the ambulance.

The guy decided to roll over. Because he was seatbelted to the stretcher and the stretcher was lifted as high as it would go, him attempt to roll over caused the stretcher to flip over, and the guy landed face first on the metal grate on the ground. This split his head wide open. The medics unbuckled him from the stretcher, turned the stretcher back right side up, and asked us to help them get him back on the stretcher. He was then pushed on the stretcher, this time with it not fully extended, to the ambulance and loaded inside. Now that he was in the ambulance, they hooked up the blood pressure and heart monitor and started treating him medically.

Once he was inside the ambulance and hooked to the monitors, my role changed without anyone saying it out loud. He was still in my custody, and whatever happened next would follow me, whether I had caused it or not.

The medic who was treating him said he needed a deputy to ride in the ambulance with him to the hospital. We did not have any criminal charges on him, but I rode with the ambulance to the hospital anyway because my handcuffs were on him just in case he woke up and started tearing up things or fighting with the medics. The medic treating him said he was in SVT or super ventricle tachycardia. He had the other medic start driving toward the hospital.

While the ambulance was leaving the driveway of this house, I heard the sound of scraping down the side of the ambulance; it turned out to be the ambulance running over the water main for the house. It was like I was in a book. There was no way all these things came together in a perfect storm and were all happening together, but they were.

It felt like one of those moments you don't talk about on the job. When too many things line up at once, when coincidences start stacking instead of spreading out, you don't call it bad luck; you just brace yourself and keep moving.

Police officers, firefighters, nurses, and EMS workers are a very superstitious group of people. If you ever want to make one of them mad, say the word "quiet" around them, especially, "It sure is quiet today." You'll get dirty looks or, worse, cussed out for uttering the unmentionable phrase. Years on the job teach you that when things stack up too neatly, too many coincidences, too many moving parts, it's usually a warning, not luck. You never say it out loud.

Well, I guess just thinking an unmentionable phrase was good enough. The medic treating the man pulled out a large binder and began looking up the protocol for SVT. The protocol he found told him to administer adenosine to correct the SVT. He administered one dose of the medication and asked me to time it and tell him when two minutes had passed. After the two minutes passed, he administered a second dose of the same medication. I found out later that this medic was not a paramedic but an intermediate medic and from what I have been told by medical staff, he was operating in a gray area of his license where he probably should not have been operating. We were still over an hour away from the hospital. The medic did not do anything else to the guy except watch his vital signs as we just kept rolling down the road to the hospital.

We arrived at the hospital around 5 a.m. and parked in the ambulance bay at the hospital. The medic began taking off the heart monitor and blood pressure cuff. Once those things were off, he got out of the back of the ambulance to take him inside the hospital. While he was getting out, I saw the guy's eyes open up. He sat up slightly and took a deep breath. The man then slumped back into the position he had been in for the whole ride. I had to alert the medic that he needed to check on the guy. He said a couple choice words and got back in the ambulance. He then started CPR on the man. Nurses started to pour out of the emergency room to assist him with CPR. One nurse even got on top of the stretcher and was doing CPR as they wheeled the stretcher toward the trauma room. They did CPR on the guy for around thirty minutes, but were unable to resuscitate him.

When they stopped CPR, the room went quiet in a way that felt heavier than the noise had been. There was no announcement, no dramatic moment; just a subtle shift in posture, the understanding that this man was not coming back. A few hours earlier, he had been alive, violent, and unpredictable. Now he was still, and I knew the scene had changed.

I now had a problem. My handcuffs were still on him. Since my handcuffs were on him the death was ruled a death in custody, and an investigation would have to be done. I notified my command staff at the sheriff's office and then called TMPA for assistance from an attorney. I was now stuck at the hospital until detectives from my agency showed up to start the investigation. They also had to call the Texas Rangers to investigate it, too.

The flood of thoughts come at times like this through an officer's head. I knew I had done everything in my power to help this guy, but it seemed like the system let him down. It's very frustrating to know things were done so poorly from the EMS response. I discussed this incident with every medic I knew, and they all came to the same conclusion: It sounds like a methamphetamine overdose, and the correct course of action would have been an IV of saline water and a trip to the hospital; nothing more could be done for him.

Knowing that didn't make it easier to sit with. I kept replaying the call in my head, walking back moments where something might have been done differently. That's the part people don't see—the quiet accounting that starts once the scene is over. You don't get to hand that off to anyone else. You carry it, whether the outcome was inevitable or not.

Everyone I talked to was in shock that the medic gave adenosine. I never saw these two medics after this call. I was told the medic that gave the adenosine would face sanctions with the state due to his actions, but I have looked for confirmation of this, and it does not show any actions against his license. The EMS company eventually either went out of business or was purchased by another company. There was some relief that the family did not have to have code words anymore because they feared their son, but I cannot fathom how they must feel seeing the ineptitude from the response of the medics that night. I know the guys I worked with all made a pact that if this ambulance company ever showed up to work on us, we would just take our partner to the hospital ourselves and would not allow them to touch us for anything other than a minor injury.

The attorney from TMPA had me email him my report before I submitted it to the department. The attorney read my report and did not think I had anything that needed to be addressed that I hadn't already covered with the report. His only comment was that the ambulance company would have a really bad day. It normally isn't a good thing when you are being investigated by the Texas Rangers. I was worn out, but I found it difficult to fall asleep during this time with the looming investigation. Thankfully, the Rangers did not have any questions for me after reading my report, and I was cleared of any wrongdoing in the case.

CHAPTER THIRTY TWO

SHOT BY A FRIEND

I WAS ON PATROL ONE EVENING WHEN THERE WAS A call about a person shot. I was not the primary deputy who responded to this call but the second or third deputy to arrive. When I arrived, I walked toward the front of the trailer house; the other deputy was already on the front porch. That's when I saw a preteen boy lying on the front porch. This boy could not have been older than thirteen years old. All I could picture was my nephew in Dallas who was the same age and same skin tone. That was the hardest part. A little piece of me connected with the whole scene, as it could have been my nephew on the porch.

It was obvious he was dead. There was a hole in his mouth and the back half of his head was missing. The strangest thing was the kid's teeth were inside the trailer house while he was lying on the front porch. The blow back of force had pushed his teeth the opposite way. It is just one of those scenes that I will never forget. When the detectives arrived on scene to investigate the death, I was cleared to go back to work.

What was told to me by the primary officer for the investigation was that the dead kid's best friend had been playing with his father's hunting rifle. He did not know it was loaded and accidentally fired the shot that hit his best friend in the face, causing his death.

This tragic incident changed the lives of so many people. I don't have the answers to what happened next, and I don't know what grief the kid who pulled the trigger lives with now. I don't know the emptiness the family must feel at the loss of this child. What I do know is things crumbled for two families that night, and I know it only takes a split second to change your world. It seems like that's why when I looked at the child, I saw my nephew. I knew my world could have been the one in pieces that night.

CHAPTER THIRTY THREE

EIGHTEEN-WHEELER VS. TRUCK

IT WAS ONE OF THOSE NAUGHTY WORD (SLOW AND QUIet) type of nights. I was headed to the sheriff's office to finish up some paperwork before heading down to have breakfast with my crew and the Lumberton PD guys to end the shift. It was about 3 a.m., and it was a dark night. The clouds were covering the moon and stars, and everywhere that did not have artificial lighting was pitch black.

Dispatch called for a trooper. It was about the time he was getting off work so he was already headed to the house. You know as soon as they ask for a trooper on the radio, the next thing they are going to say is there is an accident at some location in the county. Dispatch said there was a major accident just south of the county seat of Kountze between an eighteen-wheeler and a truck. Major accident denotes there is someone injured at the scene from the accident. It was only about five miles from where I was, so I responded, and there I was driving south on U.S. 69 out of Kountze toward this accident. My general rule for myself was 20 mph over the speed limit if going to an incident that involved someone hurt or about to get hurt. Being that the dispatcher had already said it was a major accident, I knew someone was hurt. The speed limit was 70 mph so I was going 90 mph.

When I got close to the intersection dispatch had given, I began to slow down and scan the front windshield for any wrecked vehicles, but I could not see anything resembling a wreck. There was an eighteen-wheeler stopped on the shoulder of the road up ahead so that must be where the wreck was. Then out of nowhere, I passed a truck in the middle of the road missing its whole wheel assembly on the front while and the rear end of the truck was twisted out the back. My thoughts were, *Man, that truck is torn up, where is the driver?* At the same time, I slammed on the brakes, attempting to stop while passing this torn-up truck.

Wrecks like this don't announce themselves. They scatter clues in pieces, and you have to start sorting them while your body is still reacting. I knew before I fully stopped that whoever had been driving that truck hadn't walked away unharmed.

There was someone in the cab of the eighteen-wheeler who was waving his arms, attempting to get my attention. Was that the driver of the eighteen-wheeler or of this truck? I got out of my vehicle and walked up to the man flagging me down. He told me I needed to go check on the driver of the truck. I asked where they were? He then pointed to the truck. As I got closer to the truck, I saw a huge pool of liquid under the truck. With the way the truck looked, that pool could be anything: oil, transmission fluid, antifreeze.

I found the driver still behind the steering wheel of the truck. She was in a semi-conscious, mostly unconscious state, but she was alive. She had cuts going almost completely up her left arm. She had cuts on her face and was missing teeth. There was blood everywhere. She was wearing the uniform for an industrial electrical company and had tattoos that represented the U.S. military. I got on the radio to give dispatch the information about who was hurt and the seriousness of the injury so that the ambulance crew could be prepared, and they could get a medical helicopter headed our way. You don't get much training besides CPR as a police officer, but it was obvious this lady was breathing and did not need CPR. I thought to myself, *I hope the ambulance is close by.*

When you're standing over someone who is badly hurt, knowing they're alive, knowing they need help you can't provide, all you can do is watch their breathing, keep talking to dispatch, and hope the next set of headlights shows up in time.

It was about this time that the trooper arrived on scene. He stopped to assist me before starting all the paperwork that was involved for these accidents. The trooper took one look at the lady and said she needed a tourniquet on her left arm. I thought to myself, *How stupid of me not to think about applying a tourniquet to her arm, I had one on my belt.* I also thought about how much pain the squeezing of that tourniquet on that severely mutilated arm was going to hurt.

I knew there was no way around it. Stopping the bleeding meant causing intense and deliberate pain, and I hated it. However, you don't get to soften it or ease into it. Sometimes saving a life means hurting someone worse than they already have been hurt. You have to make that decision without flinching.

I went to the passenger side of the truck and opened the door, climbing into the truck with the female. The trooper finished getting the tourniquet around her arm, and he started turning the lever to squeeze down on the arm to cut the blood flow off. As the trooper turned the lever, I had the lady look at me and not at her arm. I extended my right hand and told her to squeeze it as tight as she could to help with the pain we were about to inflict on her in an attempt to save her life. She initially did not take my hand. But after a couple turns of that lever, you could tell it was causing serious amounts of pain. The lady started trying to get away from the pain by pushing up with her legs. She then reached out, grabbed my right hand, and squeezed as hard as she could.

Her grip was pure instinct, the kind that doesn't ask permission or care who you are. In that moment, I wasn't a deputy, and she wasn't a patient. We were just two people bracing against pain, holding on because letting go wasn't an option.

I placed my left arm across her legs and used my body weight to keep her still. By this time, the trooper had finished tightening the tourniquet and the lady passed out from the pain.

It did not take long for the ambulance to arrive and begin treating this lady. They moved her from the truck into the back of the ambulance to work on her while they waited for the medical helicopter to arrive. While the ambulance crew worked on the lady in the back of the ambulance, the trooper began the paperwork for the accident report, which I assisted him with. It turned out the lady had just gotten off work for the electrical company and was headed northbound on U.S. 69 going home to Kountze. She had fallen asleep behind the steering wheel and had drifted across the center median and into oncoming traffic. She barely side swiped the eighteen-wheeler truck itself, but the tanker trailer it was pulling had sheet metal fenders that covered the rear wheels of the eighteen-wheeler truck.

The driver side fender had come through the windshield of that truck. It was like a can opener on the truck's driver side, and the fender was almost like a knife on the arm of the lady, tearing portions of her arm from wrist to shoulder.

When the medical helicopter landed in the middle of the highway, they flew her straight to a hospital in Beaumont and then flew her again to a hospital in Houston. When the helicopter left with her, we did not think there was much of a chance she was going to make it all the way to the hospital. The tourniquet remained on her arm the entire time. The paramedic that was working on the ambulance came up to us and asked who had put the tourniquet on her. The trooper was given all the credit for that one. The medic said it was a good thing that the tourniquet was applied; if not, she probably would have bled out before the ambulance arrived. I was proud that we kept her alive and also ashamed because I had not placed the tourniquet on her as soon as I noticed her injuries.

When the medic opened the rear of the ambulance, all we saw was blood that covered the floor of the ambulance. They actually had the fire department use a fire hose off the fire truck to wash out the blood from the rear of the ambulance.

I wondered if the lady lived the whole drive home after getting off shift. I went to sleep as soon as I got home but when I woke up, I scrolled through posts on social media. I located a post that talked about the wreck and was asking for prayers for the lady. It also gave a link to her profile. I said a prayer and started to follow the post, since it was giving updates on her status. A few months later, the lady was recovering from the devastating injuries she had received. I hesitantly sent her a message, explaining who I was and apologizing for all the pain we inflicted on her. She sent me back a message telling me not to apologize and if it had not been for that tourniquet, she would have died. She was overly appreciative of it. About a year later, I was able to have lunch with her and as far as I could tell, she had just about completely recovered from the injuries.

One of the things that is hard to get used to when you first start policing is that you rarely get to see the ending of things. You show up, you do your thing, and then you leave, off to the next call. When you arrest someone, you drop them off at jail. Ninety-five percent of cases are handled outside of a courtroom. They either plead guilty or the prosecutor drops the charges. You don't ever find out what the verdict was with the case. You just move on. The same thing goes with the victims of crime, victims of vehicle accidents and their family and friends.

In this case, I was able to talk to the lady for the next year or so. I was able to see the recovery. This is rare, but it should not be as rare as it is. My guess is we are all too caught up in the next thing to focus on the things we have already placed in the past. You don't get closure; you just carry the memory and move on. In this case, I was given something rare; the chance to see recovery, to know that the pain I witnessed didn't end there. Most officers don't get that; most never find out how the story ends.

CHAPTER THIRTY FOUR

GAME WARDENS

WORKING WITH THE GAME WARDENS WAS ALWAYS IN-
teresting. I have to say sometimes they do some amazing investigations. One night, I was dispatched to a 911 call about shots being
fired in a rural area of the county. When I showed up, there was no
one around. I did see a bunch of deer in the woods, so I sent a text
message to a game warden and figured that the shots they heard were
from someone who was illegally hunting deer. I did not think anything about it and went home and went to sleep.

When I woke up, I saw a text from the game warden. It read,
Thanks for the tip, I solved the case. It was an illegal hunter. I almost
dropped my phone. Caught him? From one little text about a gunshot
in the woods? I immediately called him and asked how exactly he was
able to figure out who did it from such little information. He told me
in the daylight, he was able to locate the exact area where a deer had
been killed. He also found a pocket knife beside the area the deer was

killed at. He went to a known poacher from the area and sat the pocket knife down on a bench. He asked the poacher about any recent kills he had made. The poacher acknowledged a recent kill, and the game warden asked him to show it to him.

The guy walked out to show the game warden his recent kill when he saw his pocket knife. He made a comment about finally finding his pocket knife and that's how he was caught. The man confessed to hunting illegally at night and that he had shot the deer at night. Just amazing investigative work and maybe some good luck. When the game warden told me that story, I just shook my head in amazement and laughed. It's hard for me to believe he caught the guy regardless of the way he did it. The way he did it was just brilliant.

It wasn't luck that caught him; it was patience. The kind that comes from knowing your terrain, knowing your people, and understanding that most mistakes aren't made under pressure but afterward, when someone thinks the moment has passed. The warden didn't chase a suspect; he let the truth walk itself back into the room.

Some of the other times I have worked with the game wardens were on people who got lost or had an emergency in one of the creeks in the area. We had a group of people who decided to jump in and float from one bridge to another bridge. Typically, that float takes a few hours, but the water was super high and swollen from all the rain we had received. The creek was so high, no one should have been floating the river; it was dangerous. Not to mention they decided to do this right before sunset. My first phone call was to the game wardens for assistance with a boat to help locate these people. The fire department also brought out their boat. The people were found clinging to a tree.

Another time I was dispatched to a deer that was stumbling around and running into cars. Imagine a super drunk deer, hardly able to stand, falling over when it ran, ping-ponging off parked cars. It was obvious there was a problem with the deer. I did not know if the deer had rabies or some other ailment. All I knew is it was not acting right.

Calls like this sit in a strange place, somewhere between absurd and dangerous. On the surface, it's almost comical, but underneath, it's a reminder that unpredictability doesn't announce itself. You don't get to decide what matters based on how ridiculous it looks. You treat it seriously because the consequences of being wrong are real. Policing teaches you quickly that dismissing something because it seems harmless is usually how people get hurt.

It was the middle of the night, and a homeowner called in because he heard someone outside messing with his parked car. There was no one more qualified to handle this situation than a game warden. I whipped out my cell phone and started making the phone calls. That's when I hit a snag. No one was answering. I ended up having to call the 800 number to report poachers. They were able to make contact with one of the game wardens from my area, and he came out and met me. He also brought a small caliber rifle with him, which worked really well since we were in a neighborhood. The theory was that the deer got hit by a vehicle and was in a bad place and suffering. The deer was laying down next to a house. Every time we moved toward it, it would get up and stumble off to get away from us. The decision was made to put down the deer before it damaged any other vehicles or hurt itself further.

I also got to go help them with some boating while intoxicated (BWI) enforcement; it's almost the same thing as a DWI. They even allowed me to drive their big boat on the river. That thing was so fast, and I had so much fun out there on the water. They actually caught a BWI too, but ended up not charging the guy due to some technicalities. I personally have never had a bad experience with the game wardens. They are a group who don't play when it comes to wildlife laws and safety on the water, but they always were on the up and up.

Working around people like that mattered more than I realized at the time. When systems function the way they're supposed to, when everyone knows their role and does their jobs, it creates a sense of stability you start to depend on. You don't notice it while it's there. You only feel it when it's about to be tested or torn apart.

CHAPTER THIRTY FIVE

HURRICANE HARVEY

IN AUGUST OF 2017, HURRICANE HARVEY DEVASTATED the coastline of Texas. The initial impact of happened several hundred miles from where I lived in the southeast corner of Texas at the Louisiana line. No one thought it was going to have a major impact on my area, but it had other plans. Hurricane Harvey made landfall three times within a six-day period and caused approximately $125 billion in damage and dumped more than twenty-seven trillion gallons of rain on Texas.[1]

Harvey stalled once it had made landfall and began dumping massive amounts of rain on the east side of the storm, eventually re-emerging into the Gulf of Mexico where it continued to gain tropical moisture, fueling its rain. Harvey spent about a week continuously dumping rain. In that time, the area I was in got some 5'6" of rain.

I was working night shift during Harvey. At the beginning of Harvey it was just a rain event, and southeast Texas is no stranger to

---

1   See TDEM, "HURRICANE HARVEY DR 4332," https://www.tdem.texas.gov/disasters/hurricane-harvey.

rain events. It was about 1 p.m. and I was sound asleep in my bed when the phone rang. I squinted at my phone to see who was calling me; it was my sergeant. It's almost never a good thing when you're awakened in the middle of your night by your sergeant, who should be home sleeping the same as you are. His first question to me was, "Where are you?" I don't know how exactly I answered that, seeing that my mind was still foggy from just waking up, but I know I thought, *I'm at home in bed after working in the pouring rain all night.* That's when he told me I needed to get to Hardin County as soon as I could before I got stuck and was unable to make it to work.

I wasn't being asked if I could make it in; I was being told that if I didn't, there might not be anyone else who could. When you work in law enforcement, you learn there are days you report for duty, and days duty reports for you; this was the latter.

I asked him if it was really that bad. He told me the water was over U.S. 69, and they were monitoring it and believed they were going to have to shut down the highway at any moment, which would leave me stranded with no way to get into Hardin County.

I jumped out of bed and started packing a backpack full of clothes. If I was going to get stuck in Hardin County, I at least needed a few sets of underwear, socks, and uniforms. It was a precarious drive: the southern county line is made up of a bayou, which had already risen and was three feet or so over the highway. The water just did not end. Every low spot on the highway was covered in at least three feet of water. I would drive over an overpass, and the water would go away just to see when I topped the overpass, there was more water at the bottom. I finally made it to Lumberton which, thankfully, is mostly high ground in the area, but a majority of the area south of the city limits was underwater. It appeared that the southern part of the county was the only area at this time that was flooding.

If flooding stayed contained to one part of the county, maybe we could manage it. Maybe it would crest, recede, and turn into another story people told later about how bad the rain got. I still believed this was a problem with edges, something you could draw a line around and say, "It stops here." I would learn quickly how wrong that assumption was.

I drove north to the sheriff's office in the City of Kountze to let them know I had made it to the county and received my assignment for the night. When I got to the sheriff's office, I was told my assignment was to answer 911 calls, patrol the county, and keep an eye out on the flooding.

With all the rain and flooding, there were no 911 calls coming in, and everyone was staying home. Even with almost nine hundred square miles to patrol, things get rather boring when you and some other cops are the only people out. I called a friend who dispatched for a City Police Department in Orange County. She told me she was stuck at work. I told her I was stuck at work too, and I had to figure out where I was going to sleep. She told me her teenage kids were at her apartment and since she wasn't going to be there, I could check on her kids and stay there until we were both able to make it back home. So I went to the sheriff's office several times. I don't remember why but I was dispatched to something that required me to exit my patrol vehicle briefly in the rain.

The rain had become relentless. It wasn't letting up between calls nor was it tapering off the way storms usually do. It felt constant, heavy, patient, like it wasn't in a hurry because it didn't need to be. That was the first moment I started to wonder if this wasn't just rain anymore.

When I got back in, there wasn't a dry inch on my body, and my uniform could not absorb any more water. I went back to the sheriff's office and changed into a new set of clothes. The jail had the inmates wash and dry the set I was wearing in the jail's laundry facility.

All of the sheriff's office administration were at their homes sleeping because they all lived in the county. It was around midnight when I crossed the bridge leaving the Kountze City limits and to my surprise, the water was about six inches deep over the bridge. I notified dispatch that the water just south of the Kountze City limits was now over the road. Dispatch notified the sheriff, and all the sheriff's administration got a phone call to immediately come to the sheriff's office in Kountze. I continued my patrols and was absolutely bored out of my mind.

The rain had been steady for so long that it started to feel normal, like background noise you stop noticing. Roads that should have been safe felt familiar, predictable; that's usually when things change.

I started to head back to the sheriff's office on U.S. 69 when I hit a huge puddle of water in the road. My patrol vehicle started to hydroplane and swerve as it was sailing across the top of the water. There were no creeks or anything in this area, but somehow the water was starting to cover here, too.

When my shift was over, I went to my friend's apartment in Lumberton and went straight to sleep. By the time I woke up that afternoon, the City of Lumberton was an island; there was no escape. The sheriff's office let us know that everyone was going to be working every day for the foreseeable future. They were going to have half the department work the day shift and the other half work the night shift. They kept everyone who was already working the night shift on night shift. The county was basically cut in thirds and because of the high water, the area you were in was the area you were stuck in.

The area you were in became your world, and whatever was inside, it was your responsibility with whatever resources you had on hand. The west side of the county did not have a deputy who lived in that area so there were going to be issues getting to that area if a need for a deputy arose. The next problem was that all of us in the southeastern portion of the county had no way to get to any jail if we needed to take someone to jail. So arrests would have to be a last-resort option. We were also cut off from the hospitals in the area. Lumberton did have a free-standing emergency room but it was not equipped beyond emergency medical treatment.

The county judge instituted a mandatory curfew for this time period. Everyone had to stay inside between the hours of 8 p.m. and 7 a.m.; this made for some long nights. The day shift had to deal with water rescues and all the administrative issues with the flooding. For night shift, we were focused on looting and since people were stuck in the house with each other and having nothing to do but drink alcohol, the inevitable domestic disturbances. One of the game wardens ended up getting electrocuted during some water rescue activities: thankfully, he survived.

During the curfew period, another deputy and myself were parked driver door to driver door, talking in a parking lot, just waiting for the end of shift. It was about 3 a.m., and there was not a soul in sight besides the other deputy. It had been that way for hours. We then saw a car going by. We both looked at each other and then back at the car. The other deputy said, "Let's stop it and see why it's out driving around." The other deputy pulled behind the vehicle and turned on his emergency lights. The vehicle immediately turned on a side street and started slowing down. The vehicle then punched the gas, and we were off to the races. It turned left on the next road. This road had several twists and turns in it, and it was lined with trees.

I remember thinking there was nowhere to run. This pursuit was not going to last long and was probably going to end somewhere with water.

Much to our surprise, Harvey had caused one of the trees to fall across the road. Now someone had cut the majority of the tree up and gotten most of it out of the road, but there was a portion that was still sticking out into the road from the right shoulder of the road.

The vehicle we were pursuing had to swerve hard to the left to miss the tree in the road. This caused him to lose control of the vehicle, which rolled on its side and slammed into a row of trees. The deputy who initiated the stop on the vehicle had to slam on his brakes to avoid hitting the car. I also had to slam on the brakes and swerve to stop from hitting the rear of the other deputy's vehicle. When we came to a stop, I looked over at the fleeing car and saw the driver attempting to climb out of the vehicle but became stuck, hanging half inside and half way outside of the vehicle.

The chase was over, the adrenaline drained out, and all that was left was a man broken by his own decisions. It didn't matter why he ran or what he had done up to that point. Looking at the wreckage, I was reminded how fast a choice can turn into a consequence that can never be undone.

Within minutes, there were several Texas troopers on scene. It ended up they had gotten stuck in Lumberton along with all of us. Fire and EMS arrived on scene and got the driver of the vehicle out. The only medical location was the stand-alone emergency room. EMS transported him there. We found out later the vehicle was stolen from an elderly lady that night, but she had been sleeping and did not report it stolen until the morning. The emergency room had to call a medical helicopter to transport the suspect to a hospital in Tyler, Texas, several hours to the north of us, because the suspect had broken his back in the wreck. We filed for a warrant for his arrest for evading arrest or detention with a vehicle and for unauthorized use of a motor vehicle.

The next shift, the same deputy from the vehicle pursuit, got dispatched to a disturbance at the beginning of the shift, around 6 p.m. A guy was on a four-wheeler causing issues. When the deputy arrived, the guy on the four-wheeler was drunk and was also carrying a handgun. There was nothing the deputy could do besides arrest the man. Now we had to figure out how we were going to contain him or get him to jail. Since there was still sunlight out, the plan was that he would drive with the guy toward Kountze.

Under normal circumstances, this would have been no issue; instead, we were improvising an arrest in a county cut off by floodwaters. The jail was unreachable by normal means. It wasn't about what was ideal; it was about what was still possible.

The deputy would park his patrol vehicle at the water's edge. The Kountze Fire Department would have a boat available to ferry him across to the other side of the flooded area. Another deputy would meet this deputy at the other side of the flooded area, and they would both transport the man to jail. The deputy would quickly fill out the paperwork for jail booking and then be taken back and ferried again across the flooded area by the fire department.

When the water finally started to recede after a couple of days, the damage was unbelievable. Whole neighborhoods had to completely gut their houses. They were removing all the contents from the house and lining the roads with all their possessions, which were now garbage. You can't imagine the smell. Everything was wet with floodwaters, some of which contained sewage which was now deposited on the street. Thousands of vehicles were flooded and deemed total losses by the insurance companies. At one point, the insurance companies were giving wrecker drivers job assignments to pick up flooded vehicles but were not communicating it with the owners of the vehicles. Therefore, we were getting several reports of stolen vehicles, all of which ended up being miscommunications.

The curfew was still in effect, but the roadways were opening up. The sheriff assigned me to the very rural west side of the county. It was after 8 p.m. and there were still a lot of people out driving around. I went to one of the main residential streets where I had seen a lot of traffic. I pulled over to the side of the street and turned on my emergency lights. I stood in front of my vehicle and talked to every vehicle that came by. I gently reminded them of the curfew that the county judge had imposed. I understood that curfews were not a normal thing so I was not issuing citations or taking any legal action toward the people violating curfew, just a simple reminder of the curfew.

Enforcement wasn't about punishment; it was about presence. People were tired, displaced, and unsure of what rules still applied when so much else had disappeared. My job wasn't to escalate tension; it was to keep the peace in a county already stretched thin.

One of the vehicles that stopped had a little boy in the vehicle. He was timid with me; I guess it was the uniform. I talked with the kid and even got a junior police sticker from my vehicle and gave it to him. This excited the boy and he broke into a smile from ear to ear. He then wanted a photograph with me. He still had that big smile and was giving a thumbs up in the photograph.

One night, I was sitting at an unmanned fire station just watching for anyone out and about. Everything was still and silent. All of a sudden, I heard two or three gunshots. I got in my vehicle and started to drive up and down the streets in the neighborhood. While driving, the roar of wind did not make sense. When I looked in that direction, I saw a house fully engulfed in fire. The fire was so intense that you could feel the heat from across the street. The flames leapt out of the roof of the two-story house at about the same height as the house itself. The fire was sucking in so much oxygen that it was creating its own wind, and that wind was whipping the fires into what appeared to be a tornado coming out of the roof of the house.

I immediately knew there was nothing I could do; the fire had already taken control of the house. My role in that moment was to secure the scene and get help moving.

The gunshots I heard were from ammo within the residence that went off during the fire. This would be the first of several house fires that occurred during this period. Fortunately for the fire department, a crew from the Ft. Worth Fire Department had come down to assist with manning the fire station so the crews could have a break. Everyone had been working every day for two or three weeks at this point, and the fire crews were getting exhausted. The crew from Ft. Worth Fire, along with the Lumberton Fire Department, was able to extinguish the fire without much difficulty, but the house was completely destroyed. There were more fires to come, some with much more devastating consequences.

CHAPTER THIRTY SIX

HOUSE FIRE

A MONTH OR TWO AFTER HURRICANE HARVEY CAME through the area, I was working the night shift again. It was about 2:30 in the morning, and nothing had happened all day. It becomes dead around this time at night so again, like I have a habit of doing, I decided to drive to the north county line and patrol that area. It's pretty common in the area that people burn tree limbs and other debris, and I noticed the distinct odor of burning wood while driving around. The sky also looked foggy, which is a common occurrence near the coast. I thought nothing about these two events; both were relatively common for the area.

I continued driving to the county line and did some patrolling in the area. I was headed back south toward the city when we received a 911 call about a house fire in the area. I took off in the direction of the fire. When I arrived, I was relieved to find the house was not on fire, but an unattached garage in the rear of the house was. It was completely engulfed in flames, and every wall in the garage had fire from the bottom to the top of the garage. I went and knocked on the door to alert the homeowner to the garage fire. When the man opened the door, I explained to him that his garage was on fire. He calmly told me his daughter and grandchildren lived in an apartment in the garage. I asked him if they were home and he said he did not know. My heart sank because I knew if they were in the garage, they were not going to be alive.

The fire department arrived and started fighting the fire. Once the fire was under control, the fire department located six dead bodies. We did not know how the fire started so it became a crime scene. It was not long after this that the father of the kids arrived. I was sitting in my car when he got there. I placed my cell phone in my shirt pocket, got out of my vehicle, and approached the father. The father said he was going to see his kids, but I could not allow that to happen. The father attempted to push past me, and I had to grab onto him. Myself and another officer ended up wrestling him to the ground. The scuffle shattered the screen on my cell phone. The fire was ruled an accidental fire and was not intentionally set, which was a relief, but it was still sad that people died.

There will always be questions in the back of my mind about the smoke smell and seeing what I thought was fog, but really was the smoke from the fire. If I had searched the area at that time, would it have changed anything? All the fire department people and my later studies into arson investigations say if I could see the smoke rolling over the road like it was, the smoke had already smothered them, and there would have been no different result. I know this to be true, but there is always that doubt in the back of my mind. The doubt never asks what I did wrong; it asks what I might have done differently, and it never stops asking.

CHAPTER THIRTY SEVEN

MENTAL HEALTH

"WHOEVER BATTLES MONSTERS SHOULD SEE TO IT THAT in the process he does not become a monster himself" and "when you look long into the abyss, the abyss also looks into you," are quotes from Friedrich Nietzsche's *Beyond Good and Evil*.[2]

In the late part of 2018, the sheriff called me about the possibility of the sheriff's office starting a new mental health unit. To my knowledge, I was the only deputy employed at the sheriff's office who had been through the training as a mental health peace officer. He gave me some of the particulars of the job, which included having someone from the local mental health authority ride with the deputy. He asked me if I would be okay in a partnership like this and also asked if I would be interested in the position. I told him I was.

What I didn't say out loud was that I already knew what that job would demand. I had seen enough suffering to understand that this wasn't a role where you could stay detached. It would require patience,

---

2   These passages are found in §146; see https://www.gutenberg.org/ebooks/4363.

emotional presence, and a willingness to sit with people in their worst moments without being able to fix them. I said yes anyway, because by that point in my career, I knew that pretending those moments didn't exist wasn't an option anymore.

Several months passed, and I hadn't heard anything from the sheriff about whether it was going to happen. About a month later, I found out I was going to be starting the new position in March of 2019. This unit acts like a task force where there are several agencies that work together for the mental health of the whole area. At this time, there were four counties where each had at least one deputy assigned, as well as the City of Beaumont. Later, the area was enlarged to include another county.

The weekend before I started the position as the mental health deputy, my department got into a wild call that involved two officers shooting a suspect and the suspect being on life support at the hospital. There was about a month's worth of training I had to go through at the local mental health authority before I was able to be one of their mental health deputies. I ended up working some overtime assignments guarding the suspect at the hospital; this led me to ask myself what our department was doing for the mental health of the officers in the department. I ended up writing a proposal for people in the mental health taskforce to go to training to assist other officers when there was a critical incident.

From there, we all joined the area Critical Incident Stress Management team. I ended up doing most of my training with a deputy of the Jefferson County Sheriff's Office, Stephen Hinton. I was able to see a lot of the inner workings of the local mental health authority while riding with Deputy Hinton.

It was not long into me riding with Deputy Hinton that the topic of religion came up. Deputy Hinton asks a lot of questions; that's just his nature. I relayed to him that I was a Christian, had graduated from a Christian school, but my walk with Christ could be better. I don't know what it is about police work, but it seems to me you see the depravity of man day in and day out, and you're either drawn into a walk with Christ or pushed away. The job tries to pull you away due to shift work and other requirements. Now that I was with the mental health unit, I was working the standard workday hours rather than shift work.

Unfortunately, the Lumberton Police Department was having problems finding officers to fill some of their off-duty jobs, one of which was at a church for the services. I thought to myself, what better way to go to church than to get paid for it? Also, it holds me accountable because people were counting on me being there.

Throughout my childhood and teen years, my mother made sure I went to church. I even attended a Christian school from fifth grade until I graduated from high school. When I attended college and for the first part of my career, I was rebellious from religion. I never lost faith that Jesus was the Son of God and had died for my sins and had risen from the dead, all to, by grace, forgive me of my sins, but I was not living a life that showed anyone that I believed that. When I was fired from the university Police Department, my high school friends and I were all in the stage of life where we were getting back to going to church.

The grace that was shown to me during that stage of my life was overwhelming. It came at a time when I had very little confidence left in myself and even less clarity about where my life was headed. That grace didn't erase the consequences of my mistakes, but it did steady me enough to stop spiraling. It shifted my focus away from the chaos I had created and back toward God, not as an escape but as an anchor.

When I was hired at Lamar PD, I had a much closer walk with God, but I was still far from where I needed to be. Deputy Hinton, through careful mentorship, helped me vastly improve my walk with God, so much so that I asked him to start a prayer/Bible study before work. We had a prayer meeting and Bible study every day before work for about a year and a half until Deputy Hinton retired from the sheriff's office.

Within the first couple weeks of training with Deputy Hinton, we went to check on a person who had been very reclusive. Deputy

Hinton introduced me and I started engaging him in conversation. The guy told me his whole life story. Afterward, Steve told me how amazed he was and I was gifted because people just want to talk to me. The man had never been that open before.

Working in the mental health field, you get comfortable with uncomfortable topics. Most people have never asked someone if they were thinking about killing themselves, let alone hurting or killing other people. Even as a patrol officer, I really never asked someone if they wanted to hurt or kill someone else. I was completely shocked at how many people actually want to hurt or kill other people. You also ask people about hallucinations, and this is where things can be bizarre. The mind is a powerful thing and with hallucinations and delusions, you have to expect the unexpected.

One person I worked with believed there was a large group of people that were serial stalkers, rapists, as well as other things. She believed that a local businessman, along with several other people she knew, had all worked together to ruin her life. The woman felt that they drugged her and tortured her. She claimed they had forced her to do some of the most vile and disgusting rape acts you can imagine, including with animals, and that they had used the videos as a way to make money on the dark web.

When we asked her how she knew the things above were happening, she said they had implanted a chip in her brain and were transmitting data and video to and from her brain. At times, she would tape one eye closed to disrupt the transmission of the data. She also believed that they would fly drones in a triangular fashion above her house, collecting the information. The woman tore apart several cell phones and her vehicle in the belief that they had implanted microchips which were controlling her. She would take photos and videos of people who were supposedly following her around town, saying they even would follow her to doctor appointments in Houston. She even flew to Baltimore to evade the people following her, but she never could escape them.

Another person believed that people were coming onto her property and damaging her things. She believed it was her ex-husband, that he had come into her house and removed beams from her ceiling. When I checked her attic, I could not see anything disturbed. She also thought they were taking her clothes and changing the stitching in her clothing. Her rationale for this was all the stitching from all her clothes appeared the same and when she yanked on the shirts she was wearing, the stitches would pop, so they could not be the factory stitching and had to be done by someone else.

Another guy thought he was in the middle of a video game of a circus. He was seeing clowns and circus animals, and everyone was a part of it. He demanded that I stop pointing a gun at him. I was shocked at the accusation because my gun had been holstered on my hip the whole time. That's when he told me my hands were guns, and the positions on my hands mattered, as one position made them pop guns and in another position they were real guns. He said I kept pointing the real gun at him, and he was livid about it.

Throughout my time with the mental health unit, I got to see the worst of humanity along with some of the best of humanity. There were unforgettable moments where people decided to make the ultimate choice to kill themselves and others where I was able to talk to those contemplating suicide. There were many success stories, where I would talk to people weeks later who were on the brink, and they thanked me for being there for them.

It's not all success stories though. There was a young woman I dealt with early on in the mental health unit who described what was happening to her as seeing Armageddon in the sky above us. She said it was amazing and would just stare at the sky. She ran from me at the hospital one day, and I had to chase her for about a mile before she got tired enough to stop. Now you know I hate running; therefore, I got in my vehicle and followed her as she ran. She stopped running because she was tired and knew she was not going to outrun the vehicle. She got back in my vehicle, and I took her back to the hospital. I had to take her a few times to the hospital, as she would get out and be no better so I took her right back.

What wore me down wasn't the chaos; it was the repetition. Same drive, same doors, same paperwork. Each trip back to the hospital felt less like progress and more like how thin the system really was. I wasn't arresting her, but I wasn't saving her either. I was just keeping her alive long enough to try again, hoping one of the attempts would finally stick.

I later found out she was acting like she was taking her medication at the hospital, but she was not taking it and spitting it out as soon as the nurses left. She finally decided to take the medications and once that started, her symptoms lessened and almost went away. Later, she got a job that required her to travel. While traveling, she was unable to make her doctor appointments. She told me that as long as she was working and keeping her mind busy, she was good, but her job was not very stable, and she would get laid off for months at a time. During these times, she would call me and tell me she was not doing good and needed to get back on her medication. I always was able to fast-track her and get her an appointment with a doctor within a few days. She would randomly call me and talk to me about things going on.

One Thursday night, she called me and I was not able to pick up the phone. She left a generic voicemail saying she was just calling to see how things were going. I called her the next day, but she did not answer. Saturday morning, I got a phone call from the Lumberton Police Department saying they had talked to her in the parking lot of the church. They said something seemed off with the person, but they did not think they were a danger to themselves or others. She had told Lumberton PD she knew me so the officer just wanted to let me know. I sent her a text message, checking on her, and she never responded to my text.

When I woke up the next morning, I saw in the pass-on log that the Silsbee Police Department had worked a suicide that night. The woman had shot herself that night.

I replayed the voicemail, and read the unread text again, wondering if I could have done more. In this line of work, you're trained to act, to intervene, to fix what's in front of you. There's no training for the realization afterward that all your access, all your effort, still wasn't enough. I didn't talk about it much. I just filed it away, like so many other things, and moved on to the next call.

Another time I failed in preventing a suicide, the sheriff's office was called to the house of a woman who had in the past threatened suicide. When I arrived at the house to talk to the lady, no one was around. I knocked on her door. While knocking, I heard a gunshot from inside the house. She was found deceased in her bed with a single gunshot wound.

I have been broken by these incidents, and I learned how to build myself stronger. I have seen times I was headed toward being a monster and knew I needed to adjust myself. All these people are broken people. We all are broken people, and some people just need a helping hand to lift them up out of their despair. Whether it's through faith, medications, therapy, or some other means, everyone needs a hand to hold when things get tough.

CHAPTER THIRTY EIGHT

POLICE FUNERALS

THROUGHOUT MY CAREER, I TRIED TO ATTEND AS MANY police funerals as I could. The way I think about it is you have to honor the family of the fallen officer. The only way to show that honor is to show up to the funeral. It's a sobering experience, as you think about your family as well as the family of the fallen officer. They are almost always huge events where police from all over the country show up to pay their respects to the family. It's powerful and emotional to see people who may or may not have known a person honor them in this way.

You typically dress in class A uniform, including a hat. When I went to a Houston PD officer's funeral, I had not been issued a hat from the sheriff's office. I arrived in Houston a few hours before the funeral and when going to the church where the funeral was going to be held, I saw a store that sold western wear. The typical hat for a Texas Sheriff's Office is a cowboy hat. I purchased a Stetson silverbelly cowboy hat; I still have that hat and wear it to many formal events. You also want to make sure your uniform is without blemishes, and the creases are pressed. You make sure your shoes are shining as well. It's always a meticulous process the night before a funeral; it's how I would want people to show up if I ever died in the line of duty.

The farthest and largest funeral that I have attended was in New York City. In December 2014, two NYPD officers, Rafael Ramos and Wenjian Liu, were sitting in their vehicle when someone shot them just because they were police officers. This was likely related to the Michael Brown incident in Ferguson, Missouri, and the Eric Garner case in New York City. There were protests around the country for alleged police brutality. Both the above cases were cleared through the grand jury process.

JetBlue decided they were going to support the police. The airline provided free flights to any officer who wanted to come to the funerals. I was not able to get off work for Ramos's funeral but was able to get off for Liu's funeral. I made contact with the 113th precinct of NYPD who was near the airport and helped arrange officers coming and going for funerals. They provided a point of contact and the hotel where officers from around the country would be staying.

I packed a large duffel bag full of my class A uniform and all my gear. The weight of the bag surpassed the weight of a standard checked bag. There is a process to carry a firearm on a plane, even if it's in checked baggage. The process isn't super difficult; it just requires locks and packaging for your ammunition. You then have to declare that the firearm is in your checked baggage. Once you declare it, it's checked by the Transportation Security Administration and you are allowed into the airport. While waiting at the gate for the flight, I met several other officers from around the state who were also flying to New York for the funeral. When we arrived in New York City, it was late at night. We called the 113th Precinct, and they had someone meet us at the airport and give us a ride to the hotel. As much as we were impressed with big city policing, it seemed the officers of the NYPD wanted to know how policing went in Texas. We talked to them the whole way to the hotel.

NYPD was providing a shuttle to 113th in the morning before providing buses to the funeral from the precinct house. When we were bused to the funeral, the buses had to drop us off several blocks from the funeral home. The streets were lined with police officers from all over; there were even some from Canada. Police motorcycles lined the street as far as you could see. We never made it to the funeral home. There were officers lined up in the streets several blocks from the funeral home. We lined up and stood at attention for over an hour. It's painful standing at attention for that long. When the mayor began talking, some of the NYPD officers turned their back on the mayor to show their disapproval for his stance in the ongoing controversy.

When we were leaving the funeral, several NYPD officers came up to us and thanked us for showing our respects for their fallen officer. A NYPD auxiliary officer asked us what our plans were for the rest of our time in NYC. We told him our flight was in the afternoon the next day and that we planned to see some of the sights in NYC before we left. He offered to show us around the city that night. We traded phone numbers and were able to see the Empire State Building, Times Square, and several other must-sees in NYC.

In October of 2015, another NYPD officer was killed in the line of duty and I again had the opportunity to go to NYC for the funeral. I called the auxiliary officer and told him I was coming out for that funeral. The officer provided me with a place to stay the whole time I was in NYC. He also took me around to more sights during the evenings. He had to work during the day so I roamed around the city by myself. I was able to meet several other officers from Texas at this funeral, and we still are in communication to this day.

One of the hardest things to hear at a police funeral is when the children of the fallen get up and talk. They tell you about all the things their loved one did for them and how they are not going to be around to do that with them anymore.

When the children speak about their fallen father or mother, it forces a kind of reckoning you can't avoid. You stop hearing it as a ceremony, and start hearing it as a warning. You picture your own family and the things you promise yourself you'll get around to someday. In that moment, the uniform feels heavier. You are no longer standing there as just another officer paying respects; you're standing there as someone who understands how thin the line really is between showing up for duty and never coming home again.

There are four things you hear at police funerals that you typically don't see at other funerals: the bagpipes playing "Amazing Grace," the twenty-one gun salute, the playing of taps, and the last call. Those things make the most stoic officer melt on the inside, and it takes everything we have to hold it in.

The last call is when the dispatcher calls the radio number of the officer with no answer. The dispatcher again calls the number and again no answer. After a short pause, the dispatcher or the head of the agency comes on the radio and says their radio number, date of end of watch, and signs them off forever. This is one of the hardest things to listen to, I can't fathom how hard it must be to actually do.

A police funeral represents the ultimate human sacrifice. John 15:13 (NLT) tells us there is no greater love than to lay down one's life for one's friend. I always reflect on this verse when preparing for a funeral. You have to think about what it all means. Police funerals honor the dead and warn the living. They remind every cop that tomorrow is not promised, and the real question is whether you go ready, spiritually and emotionally, when that day comes.

CHAPTER THIRTY NINE

SUICIDE IN PROGRESS

ONE DAY, TWO PATROL DEPUTIES WERE CALLED TO A house of a man who had sent text messages to his ex saying he was in the backyard with a gun and knife and was going to kill himself. Dispatch also called me to go to the scene. He told his ex if anyone showed up at the house, he would immediately shoot himself.

I met with the patrol guys several blocks away, and we formulated a plan that I was going to contact the person by phone and they would keep an eye out for him coming out of the house. We then proceeded to go to the house and parked a few houses down from the house. Once we were in place, I attempted a phone call to him. Much to my surprise, he answered the phone, and we started talking.

I introduced myself by my first name and told him I heard he was having a bad day. He told me he had already taken pills to overdose and had cut himself with a knife and that if anyone came to the house, he was going to shoot himself. I knew at this moment that we needed to get an ambulance to stage down the street and was able to relay that message to one of the other deputies. I asked him what caused him to want to take his life. He told me he had done everything he could for his children and had taken care of his children to the best of his ability. One of his children had told him recently that they did not want to live with him, but wanted to stay with the other parent. He said the other parent had poisoned the kid against him and that he did not know how to be a better parent. Since he did not know how to do anything better than what he was already doing, he was going to kill himself.

While talking to him, the man said he wanted to speak with his father. I thought to myself that I could not allow this, but could use it as a way to get him to come out of the backyard. His father had already shown up at the house and was talking to some of the officers. I could see the father talking to some of the other officers about twenty yards away from me. I told him if he put down the knife and gun and walked to the street with his hands in the air, I would allow him to speak to his father. I did not want him coming out of the backyard still armed and causing the deputies to have to engage with an armed suspect.

The man told me he was not going to come out of the backyard. He said as soon as he came out of the backyard, he was going to be arrested, handcuffed, and put in a straitjacket. He said he was not going back to a nuthouse. I told him that he was going to have to go to an emergency room because he had already overdosed on pills and cut himself. I explained to him I could not guarantee that he would not go to the behavioral hospital, and that decision would be left to the doctor at the emergency room. Then, I shared with him he would not be placed in a straitjacket. He told me he was not going to come out of the backyard. I attempted to reassure him that I just wanted to get him help, since he had already cut himself and overdosed. He said he did not want help, and he just wanted to die.

He stopped talking for a minute or so, and I heard a noise that sounded like the rattle of a pill bottle. I asked him what the sound I just heard was, and he told me it was his medication and that he just took more before he shot and killed himself. I thought to myself maybe he will pass out from taking all the medication he took, and he will be able to get to him and no one would get hurt. I continued to talk to him about his child. He said he was going to lose custody of his child no matter what because he had threatened to kill himself. I tried to reassure him that the system does not work that way.

The man continued to ask to speak with his father and was told that I was more than happy to allow him to talk to his father if he came out unarmed. He again told me he was not coming out of the backyard and his plan was to kill himself.

While we were talking, it seemed like he started to feel the effects of the medication he had taken. His speech began to slow down and was slightly slurred. He asked again to speak with his father. I gave him again the same plan as a way to speak to his father. He told me he wanted to tell his father he was sorry for everything and that he loved him before he killed himself. I told him he could tell his father himself if he just came out of the backyard unarmed. He again said he was not coming out of the backyard. The conversation continued, and I could tell the pills were starting to take effect. I started asking him about his other children, and he started to tell me about them. He told me he knew I was just trying to calm him down so he would come out of the backyard and that it was not going to work.

After about an hour, he stopped talking to me, and I started hearing a lot of noise. I heard a bunch of grunting on the phone and the sound of him in pain. I asked him what was happening. He told me I did not care about him, to which I told him I did care about him and wanted to get him some help. He stated me again that I did not care about him and if I did care, I would have stopped him from doing what he just did to himself; I did not know what he had just done to himself and told him so. He said, "Tell my father I love him and I am sorry." I then heard a gunshot. Everything went silent after the shot. I closed my eyes and took a deep breath in. I called him by name a couple times and did not hear anything else.

The other officers who were able to see him confirmed that he had shot himself in the head. I later found out from the other officers that the grunts I had heard on the phone was him taking the knife and slitting his throat. They told me he sliced his throat in one direction. He then turned the knife over and sliced his throat in the opposite direction. He told me he took a huge puff on a vape and then shot himself.

The air was heavy, but I could hear the chatter on the radio that he was still breathing, and the other deputies were moving in to assist him. I was left to deal with the father who, by this point, had gotten back into his vehicle and was sitting waiting for answers. The father saw the deputies all moving toward the backyard where he knew his son was at. The father exited his vehicle and asked me what was happening. I told him to take a seat, and I would explain what was happening. I then had to tell him that his son had shot himself. He took a huge breath and exclaimed, "WHAT?"

That single word hung in the air between us; it wasn't a question as much as it was disbelief trying to buy time. I could see his mind scrambling for some other explanation, some version of events where this didn't end the way it had. In moments like that, there's no right language, only the weight of what you know pressing against someone who isn't ready to hear it.

I then calmly explained to him again that his son had shot himself. I added the detail that he was still breathing and that EMS was coming to assist him. It took what seemed like forever for deputies to secure the scene and EMS to assist the man and transport him to the hospital. I stayed with the father the whole time. I also got the father to call someone to come be there with him.

This call was super hard to deal with. Trying to break through with someone and get them to let you help is exhausting in itself; doing that with this negative ending exacerbates the exhaustion. Having to deal with the father added an additional layer of difficulty. I was ready for the day to be over and just wanted to sleep. I replayed everything that was said several times, looking to see if I could have said anything different and whether that would have changed the outcome.

Once the ambulance reached the hospital, there was nothing the doctors could do to save this man. He was pronounced deceased at the hospital.

There was no paperwork that could have made it cleaner, no explanation that made it sit right. A man was gone. A family was shattered. The questions came from the quiet moments afterward. The noise had faded, and the weight settled in. Calls like this don't end when the radio traffic stops. They follow you home, as you replay them when the lights are off and you ask yourself questions you were never trained to answer.

CHAPTER FORTY

THE EIGHT-YEAR-OLD

I WALKED INTO THE HOSPITAL TO TALK TO A LITTLE BOY who was in the children's wing of the behavioral hospital. I had a female mental health professional with me at the time. We had gotten a referral to speak with him because at eight years old, he had attempted to poison his family. We entered and were escorted to the children's wing of the hospital. They brought this little boy to us and took us to the playroom to talk. While walking to the playroom, the boy looked at my partner and told her how pretty her eyes and smile were. He looked over to me and said I looked strong. The boy was smiling ear to ear.

When we got to the playroom, we asked him why he was at the hospital, but he did not want to talk about that. Every time we would ask him another question, he would ask if our time was up yet so he could go watch TV. It was such a strange interaction, a little unnerving really. It felt like he was just trying to manipulate us right from the start. I asked the nurses about the story surrounding the boy and read documentation on it.

The boy and his brother were adopted from foster care after their mother lost custody of them due to drug use. They thought the mother probably was using drugs during pregnancy. The family that adopted the two had had the children since they were very young. The family found it odd that recently when they cooked food, the child would refuse to eat. They figured out that the boy had been placing dishwashing soap in their meat in an attempt to poison them. The family also found out the eight-year-old had recruited the other adopted child to the mission. The hatred seemed to be directed at the mother and not the father.

After the attempted killing of the adopted parents, they did not want the children back again. I believe the state of Texas placed the children back into foster care; this was one of the oddest cases I have ever worked. It was scary and a bit horrific that someone as young as eight years old could attempt to execute a plan to kill their parents. I believe this incident also helped cause the divorce of the parents in this case. Children are normally thought of as being a blessing; in this case, the children seemed to bring such darkness.

I struggle to make sense of that darkness. We want evil to come from broken adults with long histories of abuse and neglect, but this didn't seem to fit that pattern. There was no clean narrative that made it any easier to accept. It forced me to confront the uncomfortable truth; darkness doesn't arrive fully formed. Sometimes it grows quietly, unnoticed, even inside places meant to offer safety and love. That case stayed with me because of the assumptions about innocence, responsibility, and how early damage can shape a life long before anyone knows to intervene.

CHAPTER FORTY ONE

BILL MCKEON

IT WAS THE WEEK OF MEMORIAL DAY IN 2019. I HAD gone to Dallas to be with family and friends. I just finished the weekend and got home; I had not been home for more than an hour when I got a phone call from a friend that was dispatching for the Bridge City Police Department. In that call, I only remember being asked one question, "What's going on with the officer shot in Sour Lake?" I did not have a clue, but now I wanted to know. Of course, with him calling me about an agency that was not even in the same county I worked for, I figured it was something that happened over the weekend while I was out of town.

It felt unfinished, as I stood there for a moment, I knew whatever had happened wasn't staying contained.

I had passed through Sour Lake on my way home not more than an hour beforehand, and nothing looked out of place. There was no hustle and bustle that you see in small towns when things are happening. I called dispatch to figure out what I missed. Now there's only five or six dispatchers total who work at the sheriff's office, I know them all and have talked to all of them on the phone. However, I did not have a clue who the man who answered the phone was, and to this day, I still only know he was a jailer at the sheriff's office.

I identified myself and asked if an officer or deputy had been shot in Sour Lake. He started to tell me what was happening when I heard a dispatcher in the background ask him who he was talking to. Obviously, they did not want people or the news media knowing the details of an active scene. Once she figured out it was me, he was able to tell me that Officer Bill McKeon had been shot in the face and was about to be taken by helicopter to a local hospital. The suspect was still on the run, and the sheriff's office was actively hunting him. I knew I could not just stay at home. I quickly got dressed, jumped into my work vehicle, and started that way.

Law enforcement teaches you how to move toward danger, but it doesn't always teach you what to do when the danger has passed and the damage is still unfolding. I realized that sometimes the hardest place to respond isn't to the scene, but to what comes next.

While driving, I was trying to figure out how I could best help in the situation. I was hearing the radio traffic from many agencies who were at the scene of the incident or helping with the manhunt of the suspect. The only thing I did not hear was someone going to the hospital, meeting with the family and all the things that go with that. The hospital was closer to me than the scene was anyway, and I knew the family was going to be in bad shape. Much to my surprise, the officer was not at the hospital when I arrived; this was alarming. Although I did not know exactly when this all began, it was at least a twenty-minute drive from my house to the hospital. Not to say I was following the speed limit here because I was not, but I still was not going as fast as I could muster to get there either.

Once there, it was eerily quiet in the emergency room. No one was there. Did the flight get diverted to one of the major hospitals in Houston? Did I miss something? I was waiting for what seemed like an hour until

I heard the helicopter overhead. I was still the only person there, which caught me off guard. They then brought him in. He was unrecognizable from the officer I knew. His face was puffy and swollen; this officer was a thin, old man. The guy I saw on that stretcher coming down the hall to the trauma room looked at least a hundred pounds heavier. This is when I found out Bill had not been shot, but he had been beaten.

Bradley Pruitt, a drifter, was causing a scene at one of the convenience stores in Sour Lake. The convenience store had called the police to have Pruitt removed from their property; Bill was the only officer working in Sour Lake at the time. When Bill arrived at the convenience store, he confronted Pruitt. Pruitt commenced mercilessly beating Bill, and Bill was unconscious from the beating when Pruitt disarmed him. Pruitt then shot out the window of the patrol vehicle. In the confusion, everyone assumed Pruitt had shot Bill. An off-duty officer with the Beaumont Police Department just happened to be in the area and attempted to intervene, including the use of deadly force.

Decisions are made with fragments and assumptions, and each of them carries the potential to end another life. Officers were responding to what they believed was an active threat and it was, just not exactly the way it knew at the time. It forced me to confront a hard reality: Once violence enters the scene, control is fragile and certainty is a luxury no one has.

Pruitt stole the police vehicle and was driving north on Hwy 326. Officers with the Lumberton Police Department intercepted Pruitt at FM 421 and Hwy 326. The Lumberton officers, believing Pruitt had just shot an officer, began shooting at the police vehicle driven by Pruitt. Pruitt wrecked the police vehicle and fled on foot into the woods. Officers with the Hardin County Sheriff's Office, Sour Lake Police Department, Lumberton Police Department, Texas DPS, Texas Rangers, Jefferson County Sheriff's Office, and the Beaumont Police Department descended on the area, and a massive manhunt for Pruitt began.

Meanwhile at the hospital, the doctors were working on Bill and trying to ascertain his injuries. It was not long after Bill arrived at the hospital a captain from the Jefferson County Sheriff's Office arrived. The relief of just having another person there to help bear some of the responsibility was much welcomed. Bill's family and members of the Sour Lake City Council showed up a little bit later. I watched the doctor with his hand move all of Bill's face; that's how broken the bones were in his face. You could move the whole facial structure just by touching it. They did several X-rays, and then he was placed in an MRI. The doctor believed there was going to be a traumatic brain injury associated with the trauma Bill had suffered.

I was meeting with the family and city leaders, and they were pressing me for information about his condition. I was giving them very limited information, basically that he was in fact alive and that they did not expect him to die. Since I had already been told he had a traumatic brain injury and his wife worked in the mental health arena, I told her she needed to prepare herself for the brain injury. While I was talking to them, the Texas Ranger, along with the doctor, showed up. The doctor gave them an overall picture of Bill's condition. The family asked about the possibility of a traumatic brain injury, but the doctor told the family that he did not think Bill had a traumatic brain injury. I felt angry and humiliated.

In that moment, I realized I had become the messenger of something that wasn't true. I had watched their faces change when I warned them about the brain injury, and now I could feel that trust snapping back against me. I wasn't angry because I'd been contradicted, I was angry because I had helped prepare them for a future they were now being told didn't exist. There was no way to take it back.

The doctor had confidently told me Bill had a traumatic brain injury and now was telling the family he did not have the brain injury. My credibility was on the line. How could the doctor do that to this family?

The next couple weeks, I went to the hospital several times to check on Bill's condition and how the family was doing. I wanted to make sure they felt the support of the community and the department. I also wanted to assist in any way that I could. Bill did have a traumatic brain injury, and this incident forced him to retire from law enforcement.

We rarely talk about when the injury doesn't heal cleanly. Bill didn't just lose his ability to work; he lost a part of his identity, the same one that so many of us build our entire purpose around. I couldn't help but wonder what it would look like if I was wearing his shoes. It was a reminder that this job doesn't just ask for your strength in the moment of crisis; it keeps asking, long after the call is cleared, whether you're willing to live with what it takes from you.

CHAPTER FORTY TWO

CROSSBOW

IT WAS A COUPLE WEEKS AFTER BILL'S INCIDENT. I WAS on break from a training class from the FBI on hostage negotiations when I received a phone call from a father. He was concerned about his son and some suicidal comments he had made recently. I listened to his story and provided him with some guidance about the mental health process. I also told him if his son made any more statements about killing himself, he needed to call 911 so someone could come out and evaluate his son and possibly get him to the hospital if that was warranted. After the phone call, I went on with class and had all but forgotten about it.

It was mid-morning on Thursday, June 20, 2019, the time of the day when every cop starts to wonder what is for lunch. I was at the sheriff's office, turning in paperwork for the week. The father reached out to me again this time about what his son had done last night. The father said his son had been acting very erratically. His son was living on his father's property, but not in the same house. He told me his son had come over to his house and talked about the drug cartels owning the cell phone tower located near his property. The cartels were causing electrical waves to shoot out of the cell phone tower, which was killing people.

The son also asked his father to borrow his phone because he had a special code that would disable the tower from being able to kill people. The father also said his son also made some statement about killing himself. The father stated when he woke up that morning, he found that several hay bales in his field had been set on fire. The father wanted me to come out and evaluate his son. I looked at my partner, a QMHP from the local mental health authority, and relayed to her the story I was just told. I also told her it looked like we would be having lunch in Beaumont today instead of Hardin County, as he lived a few miles west of Sour Lake.

We left from the sheriff's office and headed that way; it's approximately a thirty-minute drive to the father's house. When we arrived, the father was waiting for us at the driveway along with his ex-wife, the son's mother, and her new husband. The father urgently wanted to go check on his son. The mother, on the other hand, had a sense that something was off, and there was danger. At least that's how I felt about the energy she was putting off.

The mother said she would show me the driveway leading to her son's residence, while the father said he would meet us there. We proceeded fifty yards from the father's driveway to another driveway, which unless you knew it was a driveway, you'd never see it. It was small, and the trees were grown up around it with just enough room for a vehicle to pass through it. The mother stopped her vehicle just on the other side of this driveway. I normally don't wear my ballistic vest unless I'm going into a hot call, but due to how the mother was acting, something told me I needed to put it on. I also had the feeling that I needed to call for a backup officer.

The father was in a hurry, but the mother wasn't. She kept looking past me toward the trees, not at me, not at the road, at him. She didn't say "he's dangerous," but her body language did. That's when I knew I needed to armor up and get another unit headed my way.

I went back and forth with myself on whether I should call for a backup. I knew we were in a very rural area of the county, and if I did end up needing help, we were in a very rural area and it was going to take someone a long time to get to us. I also knew that another deputy had called out that he was doing something pretty close by and could help.

It was about this time when the dispatcher came across the radio and advised all the deputies that someone was traveling from the Batson area to Beaumont and was carrying someone who had overdosed on medication. I was still putting on my ballistic vest and preparing to go talk to this guy. I saw the mother looking at me in what I assumed was wonderment as to why I was putting on a ballistic vest. I explained to her that I felt the situation was dangerous, and I did not want to see anyone get hurt. She nodded in understanding.

I walked back to my vehicle to actually request a backup. As my hand reached out for the microphone, the dispatcher came back on the radio and dispatched the deputy who was in the area to the Sour Lake Fire Department because the person that was carrying the overdosing person had decided to stop and get medical treatment from the EMS personnel located there. I remember thinking to myself, *Great! Now backup is at least thirty minutes away.* At the same time, the father was walking down the driveway and rushing me to come check on his son.

I drove up the driveway and as soon as I got past the trees that were grown up by the road, the area opened up and revealed a large plowed field. At the front of this field was an old connex trailer. Between the connex trailer and the plowed field were two sets of trees. The set of trees on the left were a small set of four or five trees, then an open area, and on the right was a line of trees heading back toward the father's residence. The plowed field was next; it was large and flat with several round bales of hay. Those bales were charred and still had smoke rising from them. On the far-left side of the field, I observed the cell phone tower, which must be the one the father had been talking about.

The father was rushing toward the connex trailer and motioning for us to come. I parked my vehicle and got out and walked toward the trailer. The trailer was situated perpendicular to the road, and I had to walk to the opposite side of it. I noticed that a house door had been built into the door of the trailer. Unlike most house doors, this door opened outward instead of inward.

Before I got there, the father started knocking on the door. From inside the trailer, I heard a male voice, who said to go away and leave him alone. The father knocked again and attempted to open the door. The father was also saying he was there to check on him. The male voice inside said again to go away or he was going to call the sheriff's office.

I don't typically introduce myself as a sheriff's deputy because of my role with mental health, but I thought he already wanted to call the sheriff's office so I might as well tell him I was with the sheriff's office. I stood on the left side of the door and knocked on the door. I said, "Taylor, I am Deputy Lee with the Sheriff's Office, and I came to talk to you." I did not get the response I had anticipated from me announcing I was from the sheriff's office because the male voice started screaming profanities and telling me to go away. I told him I was just there to check on him and to talk to him.

Then I heard a lot of rustling from inside the trailer. Taylor said, "YOU WANT ME TO COME OUT? GET READY!" The hairs raised on the back of my neck, and my gut fell to the floor. I knew from the statement things were about to turn bad.

All of a sudden, I heard a loud bang against the door and saw the door swing open. I was on the side with the door, so I had to take a step to see around the door. When I looked at the door opening, all I saw was a crossbow pointed straight at me. My gun was holstered because I did not expect for this to happen. I started running down the side of the connex trailer while simultaneously drawing my handgun from the holster. The next few seconds were a blur. Things were moving so fast and, at the same time, it felt like they were standing still.

As my gun came out of the holster in my right hand, I began turning back toward the door. My left arm must have been up toward my face as I turned. I heard the sound of a string pop and at that instant, I felt a sunburn on my left upper arm and face.

Again, thousands of thoughts flooded my head, with the biggest question being, *Why am I now sunburned?* I also answered my own question with, *You must be shot, but how bad are you hit?* It felt like it took me a whole minute to process all of this, and it also felt like a blink of an eye. I wasn't aiming; my gun was still at my waist pointed in the general direction of the man who just shot me when I pulled the trigger. We do a similar drill every year when we qualify with our handgun; it's designed to stop someone's aggression that is right on top of you. I hadn't a clue how far he was from me, but I wanted to stop the attack.

I knew I had to go on the offensive. I had to stop him before he attacked my partner or his family. I also did not know if I was going to be out of the fight soon due to my injuries. He took off running toward the field between those two areas of trees. The connex trailer and the door blocked my view of him so I ran to the front of the trailer. When I rounded the corner, he was still running from me. I noticed him drawing a machete with his right hand; this further solidified that he was going to continue the aggression as soon as he could. I started to take aim at him as he ran away.

I don't know how it exactly happened, but as I was bringing my hand gun up to eye level to aim, another shot went off. When I finally got it to eye level, the sights were huge. I placed the front sight in the notch of the rear sight and aimed straight in the middle of his back. I pulled the trigger again.

I saw the machete go flying out of his hand and watched him crumple to the ground. I knew he was dead. I reached up to my left eye, and when I removed my hand, it was covered in blood. I reached for my radio, took it off my belt, and raised it to my mouth. My thoughts were, *Okay, he is dead, you need to stay calm so everyone doesn't race to you and cause injuries or deaths to the other deputies.* With a slow calm voice, I said, "530 Hardin County, shots fired."

There was a long silent pause on the radio. The dispatcher then asked for more information. I hit the transmit button and due to radio signal issues, which are very common in this area of the county, I just got a tone. From my right side, I saw Taylor's mother coming toward me. She pulled a handkerchief from her pocket and identified herself as a former paramedic. She looked at my face and told me it looked like a graze wound. She either handed me the handkerchief or placed it on my head and told me to keep pressure on the area. I told her to go check on her son. I knew if she was a paramedic, she had far better training for first aid than I did.

I walked toward Taylor as well. I wanted to make sure he did not have access to the weapons in case he was still alive. I noticed that the crossbow and machete were several feet from him, and he was just lying on the ground. I then walked to my vehicle and sat down. I picked up my car radio, which had more power than the handheld radio. I again told myself you need to keep it calm and give dispatch the information they need. At this point, I had no idea how long it was from the time I called shots fired until I got on the radio again. I picked up the radio and said, "530 Hardin County." Dispatch answered with my number "530." I said "530, I have been shot with an arrow. I think it's just a graze wound. I have shot him, and he is down." The dispatcher said that unit 1 (the sheriff's office) and unit 2 (the chief deputy) had been notified; the EMS service was on the way along with other units.

I spent a minute just sitting in my car, trying to gather my thoughts. I knew I needed to call the Texas Municipal Police Association and tell them I had been involved in an Officer Involved Shooting so I could get an attorney headed my way. When I called, they took my name, agency, phone number, and the reason for my call. They said the field representative would call me back shortly. I took the time while waiting for the call back to call my mother. I told her, before she saw something on the news, I had been in a shooting, and I had been shot but I was okay.

It was like time was standing still. I was waiting for EMS and other deputies to arrive. I was also waiting for a phone call back from TMPA. The mother was providing medical aid to her son, and I did not have a job to do but sit there and wait. When TMPA called back the first questions, I was asked if I was alone and if the audio/video recordings were turned off. They asked for a rundown of what occurred and then assigned Greg Cagle as my attorney. After speaking with TMPA, I continued to wait for other deputies to arrive and for EMS. Once the first deputy arrived, it started raining police.

Up until then, I had been by myself, sitting in my unit, holding it together out of necessity. When the first deputy pulled in and the rest followed, the tension I'd been carrying finally loosened its grip. The danger had passed, but the reality of what just happened was only beginning to settle in.

When the ambulance arrived, they immediately started working on Taylor; that made a few of the other guys/deputies upset that they did not check with me first and checked on the suspect, but it was not really a big deal to me. As they were walking me to the ambulance, I was approached by one of the sergeants, and he asked for my gun. I already knew this was standard procedure so with no hesitation, I gave him my gun with my holster. The EMS personnel looked over my wounds and said it appeared that nothing life-threatening happened to me, but I would probably need stitches. They wanted to know if I wanted to go to the hospital myself or for them to take me. I shrugged and deferred the question to the sheriff; after all, how I got to the hospital did not matter. While we were trying to figure out how I was going to get to the hospital, somehow everyone was figuring out it was me who had been shot. I started getting tons of messages from people on my phone. I was floored at how many people were contacting me. How did they already know? I certainly had not talked to anyone and was trying to keep a low profile.

I chose to go to the hospital by the sheriff's office instead of by ambulance. On the drive to the hospital, my phone just kept going off.

I also got the biggest headache, which I found strange. It happened at least an hour after being shot. When I walked in the door of Christus St. Elizabeth Hospital, I was met by some of the nurses, and they took me to a private room. One of the nurses who worked in the psych room saw it was me and claimed me as her patient. It only took the doctor less than five minutes before he came in to check me out. He then came back with some numbing medications and cleaned out the wound and sewed me up. In my mind, I was stitched up within the first thirty minutes of being at the hospital, which was record time if you have ever been to a hospital. I'm not sure exactly how long it took for my treatment.

My phone kept going off with messages I was not ready to answer, and my headache made it hard to focus on anything else. I realized how close I had come to not being able to walk away. I was aware that life had just changed whether I wanted it to or not.

It was not long after seeing the doctor that Buddy Rector, a field representative from TMPA, showed up at the hospital. Not long after Buddy got there, the attorney assigned to me from TMPA, Greg Cagle, arrived and got my version of the story. While discussing the story with my attorney, one of the Texas Rangers arrived. He started asking me to give a breakdown of the scene for him. My attorney immediately stepped in and told him I would not be answering any questions today. The Ranger said he just wanted to get the layout of the scene from me. That's when Greg told the Ranger that he had already been to the scene and walked the scene with the Ranger investigating the incident. He already scheduled a meeting with the Ranger and myself to give my statement, and I would not be talking to anyone from law enforcement today. The Ranger then left my room.

When the Ranger walked out, the sense of control I'd been holding onto slipped. Everything from that point forward was out of my hands, and I understood that this incident was no longer just about survival, it was about scrutiny.

I was aware that this hospital was the only trauma hospital in the area, and there was a good chance Taylor was also in this hospital getting treated for his gunshot wound. Taylor lived and spent less than a week in the hospital before he was booked into the Hardin County Jail for aggravated assault on a public servant. Greg told me in the next day or two, when I felt up to it, to start typing the details of the event and that we were going to meet with the Ranger on Wednesday of the next week to give my statement.

The adrenaline was gone, the pain was settling in, and I knew the next phase wouldn't be about what happened, it would be about how it would be judged.

After I wrote my statement, I needed to email it to him so he could proofread the statement. I was given a ride home and offered a gun from the guy giving me a ride home. I did not take his gun since I knew I had my off-duty gun at the house.

I was home by myself for an hour or so, and I just didn't feel like being alone. My head was still pounding, and now the top of my head looked like a mummy because of the bandages. I decided to go to a bar near my house and get a drink, hoping that might help the headache some and I wouldn't be alone. I knew the bartender at this bar and was asked about the bandage on my head. I gave a very brief account of what happened; I did not want to get into the weeds and be asked a lot of questions about what happened. It was not long after that the word spread around the bar, and people were walking up, shaking my hand and buying me more drinks.

The next day, the sheriff called and checked on how I was doing. I told him I was doing well. He asked me to come to the sheriff's office because he was working on a media release and wanted me to pick out a picture to include in the statement. I arrived at the sheriff's office, and the sheriff explained some of the process that was going to happen. I could not work due to the stitches in my head, which were going to be removed in a week or two. He said the Rangers would have to finish their investigation into the shooting, and they had to submit the case to the district attorney's office for review. He said that once the district attorney cleared me and my medical doctor cleared me, I would see a doctor to make sure it did not negatively affect me psychologically.

I understood then that wounds don't always announce themselves right away.

The sheriff said he expected all those things to go fine, but I would have to remain on administrative leave until they all happened. I asked him if I could go to Dallas and see my family, which he did not have a problem with. The chief deputy told me I needed to get my report finished as soon as possible. I told him I was working with my attorney to get my statement complete. He did not want to wait for the attorney and said deputies don't trust the attorneys; the only attorneys he needed were the ones up the stairs, meaning in the district attorney's office. The sheriff overheard this conversation and agreed with me that I needed to wait until I met with the Rangers and gave them my statement.

It took me a couple days before I decided to start writing about my incident. I took my computer to a local coffee shop and basically finished my rough draft while there. I did some touch-up work when I got home and sent it to my attorney. On Wednesday, I met with my attorney briefly before meeting with the Rangers. We all met at the Liberty County Courthouse where they had secured a meeting room for the meeting.

The district attorney's office refused the case without submitting it to the grand jury. About three weeks after the incident, the Sheriff called me and said I was cleared to come back to work and that he would set up an appointment with a psychologist for me to do at the sheriff's office; I got my handgun and holster back at this time. I still have the box that my handgun was put in when it was submitted to the crime laboratory, with the Texas Rangers label on it. I found out that the crossbow bolt that was used was homemade. Taylor had used a foldable tent to make a customized bolt and had fashioned the bolt out of the tent pole. He had also used a welding rod or coat hanger as the tip of the bolt.

It wasn't something bought off a shelf; it was something built for purpose. If the bolt had been hunting-grade, the outcome would've been very different.

When the psychologist met with me, he asked me to give him a brief description of the events. He asked if I had any cameras recording the interaction that day. I told him I did not have any video recordings of the incident. He seemed a little stumped by that fact and would ask me other questions and then come back to the question of why I did not have any recordings of the incident. He then pulled out the cards with the inkblots on it and asked me to tell him the images I saw on the cards. They all looked like the devil or moths/butterflies to me. I was then allowed to go back to work.

A few years had passed, and I was not even thinking about the case; you know, life goes on. I was teaching police driving at the police academy when the district attorney called me. She told me that there was a possibility of a plea agreement with Taylor and asked me how much time I wanted to see him do for his crime. At the time, I had about ten years until I was retirement eligible. I added on another five years for fifteen years. I told her I just did not want to have to deal with him again in my official capacity. She mentioned that under the law, he would have to serve at least half the time in prison. With this calculated into the equation, I agreed to a thirty-year plea agreement.

Taylor did not accept the plea agreement, and we were scheduled for court. It was almost three years to the day from the incident when we went to court. I did not sleep much that week with my mind racing about all the things I might be asked and how the defense attorney was going to twist things to make me look like the bad guy in the situation. I assumed the defense was going to take issue with the fact I shot Taylor in the back. Was my belief that he was going to continue the attack credible to the general public? There had been riots around the time of my shooting in Minnesota from a man's death where the actions of the police officer were called into question. How do you really know if the general public is going to take your side or have empathy with the suspect?

The courtroom did not scare me, but I was concerned with how I would be judged outside of it. I knew what I had seen, what I felt, and why I had pulled the trigger, but truth doesn't always travel intact once it leaves the room. I was acutely aware that public opinion doesn't operate on training, policy, or threat assessment: it operates on emotion, headlines, and hindsight. I had already seen officers across the country put on trial in the court of public opinion for the decisions they had made in a fraction of second. I wondered if people would see a deputy defending his life or reduce everything down to a single frame; a suspect shot in the back. I realize how thin the line is between being supported as a public servant and being judged as a villain, and how little control you have once your actions are no longer just yours to explain.

I was present for the whole case, but "the rule" was invoked, and I was not able to see anyone else testify. I was the first person to testify in the trial, on the stand recounting every little detail I could remember from the incident. The prosecuting attorney had just had foot surgery and had one of those wheeled scooters where he could rest his knee and was still able to move around. At one point during the questioning, he picked up the crossbow that was used against me. He held it up so I could see it and the jury was able to see it. Pointing at the wall, he asked me if Taylor had the weapon shouldered or was shooting from the hip when I saw him right after he kicked the door open. He was facing me while he was asking the question. He then turned to go back to the table where he could put the crossbow down. While turning, he pointed the crossbow at all the jury, and you could hear loud audible gasps coming from the jury members. He also had me stand with my back to the jury and simulate how I observed Taylor pulling out the machete as he ran away from me.

With my back to the jury, I reenacted those moments. I had lived this once in real time, and now I was being asked to relive it in pieces while people who had never been there tried to understand it. It was controlled and clinical, unlike the real thing.

After I testified, I was not released from the rule, even though I asked to be released. So I had to wait in the law library for everyone else to testify. It was brutal not knowing what others were saying. I was told later that the parents tried to portray me as the aggressor in the situation and that I had made a scene when knocking on the door. I was also told they tried to raise the point that in his state of mind at the time, he could not understand that I was a deputy with the sheriff's office, which I find totally absurd because to me it seemed that my introduction as a deputy is what made him blow up in the first place.

After all the testimony was over, the jury read several different charges they could convict Taylor of, from assault or assault with a deadly weapon to the most serious charge, aggravated assault on a public servant. The jury took approximately ten minutes to pick a foreman, read the charges, and find him guilty on the most serious offense of aggravated assault on a public servant. What a relief. The general public had made up their mind in no time and had sided with me.

On the next morning, the sentencing phase of the trial began. Texas has a bifurcated system, which has a trial for guilt and innocence and another trial for the punishment phase. Since the jury had already heard all the details of what happened, the sentencing phase is typically much shorter. The sentencing phase is also where the prosecution can tell the jury about previous conviction and how Taylor had already gone to prison for using a gun and threatening his mother. Aggravated assault against a public servant is a first-degree felony in Texas and holds a penalty range from five to ninety-nine years in jail. I was much less worried about what the sentence that the jury gave to Taylor for his crime. This does not negate that I still wanted him to get at least thirty years so I would not have to deal with him for the rest of my career, but I was willing to accept any sentence they gave him.

The sentence wasn't really about closure. It wasn't going to give me a sense of safety or erase the image of that day. What I wanted most wasn't a number of years; it was distance. Distance from ever having to cross paths with him, distance from carrying the responsibilities of what could have happened if things had gone differently. I wasn't waiting for justice to feel complete. I was waiting for the weight to lift, even though I already knew it wouldn't.

The jury took approximately fifteen minutes to decide the sentence of sixty years in jail, which, by my count, makes Taylor eligible for parole after thirty years. After the sentencing, I was allowed to give a victim impact statement to Taylor and to the court. I did not have a plan of what I was going to say, and I did not even know if I was going to give a statement. The crime victims advocate thought it would be best for me to give a statement. Here is what was said: "Taylor, I came to your house to help you that day. I have already said more words than you allowed me to say that day. I hope you get the help you need."

Nowadays everyone wants to know this story. They want to see the scar I will forever have above my left eye. I can't tell you how many times people have asked me to tell them about the crossbow incident. Depending on the audience, I tell it emphasizing different areas. Sometimes when I give talks on mental health, I talk about the times where I get on the highway where it happens, and I relive the event in my head. Others just want to know the action part. I rarely get to tell the whole story as I have here. Of all the things that I have gone through in this life, the week of the trial was the hardest. Not only was I going to have to relive the events that happened, but also I was going to have to face people questioning every action and reaction I did. All this was on full display for everyone to see.

The danger wasn't reliving the shooting; it was having my judgment put on trial by people who had never stood where I stood.

It really does not matter what Taylor got for his crime. I don't hold any of his actions against him. It was me who was on trial that day. The jury reached a verdict, and they sided with me. I needed that victory more than anyone else knows.

In 2022, I married the qualified mental health professional who was with me on this call. We did not even start dating until about a year after this incident. We worked every day together and dealt with some really difficult calls together. We lived in the incident when one man was hellbent on attempting to kill me. All this pulled us together and made us one.

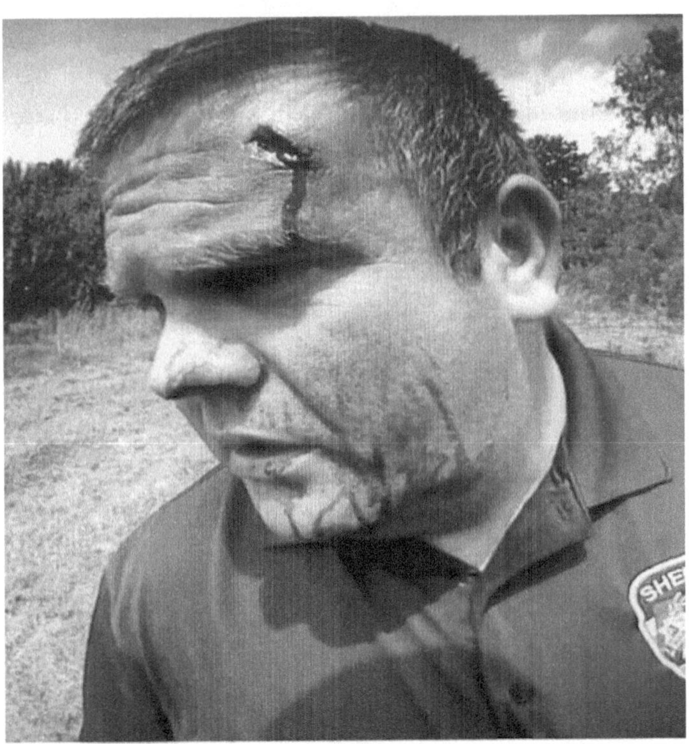

CHAPTER FORTY THREE

TYLER WILSON

ONE DAY, I WAS ASKED TO GO CHECK ON A GUY IN SOME apartments in Lumberton. The guy was unemployed and lived with his mother. When I talked to him, he told me he did not have a job after being fired from his last job for his temper. He said his temper was due to voices he heard in his head. He lived with his mother, but she was hardly at home because she drove a bus for a living. He said he wanted to get mental health help due to the voices in his head, but he did not have any way to get to the appointments. I got him set up with the local mental health authority, which got him started on a monthly shot to control the voices in his head. I had spent several months talking to him and taking him to his doctor appointments.

One day, I was walking through the sheriff's office. One of the detectives exited the interview room and asked if I could talk to a suspect who had just confessed to sexually assaulting a child. The detective never provided a name of the suspect, but pointed to the interview room. I opened the door to the interview room and, to my surprise, the guy I had been working with was in the room.

I started the conversation about his statements to the detective about killing himself. He said he knew he had done wrong, and he would have to pay a price for his actions and thinking about all that had him planning on killing himself as soon as he left the sheriff's office. The detective said she was going to submit the case to the grand jury and was not going to arrest him today so if I did not intervene, he planned on killing himself. I got him to agree that he needed to go to the hospital.

In that moment, my job wasn't to judge him or what he had done; it was to keep him alive long enough to face it.

While walking to my vehicle to take him to the hospital, he stopped me and told me to handcuff him. I handcuffed him at his request. When I inquired why he wanted to be handcuffed to go to the hospital, he told me he was thinking about taking my handgun and killing himself. I took him to the hospital and continued taking him to his doctor appointments and the appointments to receive his monthly shot.

I got a call from a detective at the Lumberton Police Department. He told me he was also investigating a sexual assault that happened in his jurisdiction and asked if I could help facilitate an interview with the suspect. I told him the Lumberton Police Department wanted to speak to him about an incident they were investigating and asked him if he would be willing to go to the interview. He agreed, and I transported him to the interview. He would not allow me to be in the interview, but the detective told me he confessed to another sexual assault of a child. The Lumberton detective said he was also going to submit the case to a grand jury and not arrest him that day. I again asked him if he was feeling suicidal. He said he was not suicidal at this time but that he knew he had done some bad stuff and he was going to have to pay the price for his misdeeds. I asked him, since he confessed, if he knew that a warrant was eventually going to be issued for his arrest, and did he want me to arrest him or one of the patrol officers. He said he wanted me to arrest him when it was time. It was an odd kind of trust, and one I didn't take lightly.

I continued to take him to his doctor appointments and to get his shot monthly. It took about six months before the grand jury returned a true bill for him and issued an arrest warrant.

The sheriff's office detective called me as soon as the warrant for his arrest was issued. They went with me to his apartment. I knocked on the door, and he answered, surprised that I was there. I told him today was the day he knew was coming and that there was a warrant for his arrest, and I was there to arrest him. He said okay and allowed me to handcuff him without any fuss. I then transported him to the Hardin County Jail. He ended up taking a plea deal for the sexual assaults and pleaded to life in prison.

I had spent months helping him get to his appointments, trying to stabilize a life that was already unraveling. In the end, the law did what it had to do, but it didn't undo the damage he caused or erase the weight of being the one who put the cuffs on him. I believe in grace, but I also wear a badge. That day reminded me that those two things don't always align and leaves you with questions no sentence can resolve.

CHAPTER FORTY FOUR

UVALDE

I WAS NOT A PART OF THE INITIAL RESPONSE TO THE school shooting, which occurred at Robb Elementary School on May 24, 2022, but a couple people from the Southeast Texas Critical Incident Stress Management (SETX CISM) had been asked to go and assist with the debriefings in Uvalde. The school shooting brought a former student to the school who shot and killed nineteen students and two teachers. Seventeen others were injured during the shooting. There is controversy surrounding the way police responded to the incident and the decision to stage for a SWAT team instead of confronting the gunman.

May 30 was Memorial Day, and I had plans to spend time in San Antonio for the holiday. I was driving on Friday night, the 27th, when a member of the team called me to give me an update on the Uvalde response. I was a fairly new president of the SETX CISM team, and the team member told me the two members of our team were assigned to the command post and were working to facilitate the response. I happened to tell him I was going to be in San Antonio for the weekend and I did not have any plans until Sunday so I would be available Saturday if they needed any assistance. He told me I should stop in and see how these operations were run just in case we had an incident in our area and had to do one ourselves. I agreed and met him at a church where they were operating at 8 a.m. that Saturday.

I drove into Uvalde at around 7:30 a.m. The streets were vacant. The sun was shining bright, but it did not seem like anyone was even in the town. It was a typical warm sunny morning in the Texas hill country. They had a briefing with everyone around 8:30 a.m. I was introduced to almost everyone before the briefing was held, but the incident commander was not available beforehand to get introduced to.

I wasn't assigned to the incident; I wasn't part of the formal response team. I was there to help carry something heavier: comfort, faith, and whatever sense of grounding could be offered in the middle of unimaginable loss. I stayed in the background, mindful that this wasn't my scene to control or direct. I was there to quietly serve, and I hoped that would be enough.

We all assembled in a classroom in the church to begin the briefing. When the incident commander walked in and saw me, she got a disgusted look on her face and started asking people who I was and why I was allowed in the room. She was told who I was and why I was there so she allowed me to stay, but things had gotten off on the wrong foot. While in the briefing, the teams who were out working at the police and fire stations said they had been asked over and over for Bibles from the first responders they had talked to. The church we were at offered all the Bibles on their shelves, but they only had a handful of Bibles available to give out.

After everything they had seen and experienced, it made sense that they were reaching for something familiar and steady. Deputy Hinton, one of the mental health deputies for Jefferson County, who was introduced earlier in this book, was also a member of the Gideon's International, the men who provide Bibles for hotels to place in the rooms around the world. I told the group that I possibly had a contact and should see if they had any Bibles they could give us so we could provide the Bibles to the first responders. They said that was a good idea so I made a phone call to Deputy Hinton. He told me he would have to check and see and would call me back in a few minutes. When he called me back, he asked if he could give my cell phone number to someone who was with the Gideons, which were located in the area we were in. Of course, I agreed to allow that. I didn't know if anything would actually come of it, but at that point, even the possibility felt worth trying.

About ten minutes later, I received a phone call from a Gideon member from the camp in the area. He asked how many Bibles we needed. I really did not have an answer for him and told him so. He said he would bring Bibles to us, and I gave him the location we were at. About thirty minutes later, he called me back and gave us three cases of Bibles. I later learned that the Gideons realized the need for Bibles to be distributed in that community after I made the phone call to them, and they were able to pass out over seven thousand Bibles to people that weekend. I assisted with mostly clerical duties for the rest of the day at the command post. The member who invited me to come and learn was later asked to leave because he did not see eye to eye with the incident commander, though the other team member stayed. Another one of our team members went to respond to the scene a week later.

At 3 p.m., I left to head back to San Antonio to be with my family, and the town had completely changed from that morning. There were people everywhere. There were vigils happening all over town. There were news crews out filming. It appeared the city had swelled in size from a few thousand to tens of thousands of people in just a few hours. When I left, I reflected on the events that happened at Robb Elementary as well as all that happened that day. I got in my vehicle and just sat there for a minute, left to ponder the whole situation. How could someone be so evil to go to an elementary school and start shooting the most innocent of people, children? The response from law enforcement and how the choices and actions of just one or a few people might have drastically changed some of the outcomes. It's all speculation and the what-ifs, where I had found myself at, in situations like the house fire. My heart hurt for everyone involved.

I wondered how evil can wear so many faces, and how sometimes it doesn't announce itself. It just walks into a school, a house, or a quiet neighborhood and shatters everything it touches. There were no answers that night, only the weight of knowing that no amount of training or authority can undo the damage. All I could do was sit with the reality that some wounds don't belong to one family or one town; they belong to all of us, and we carry them whether we want to or not.

CHAPTER FORTY FIVE

THE GIDEONS

AFTER A MASS CASUALTY EVENT, THERE IS A MOMENT no one prepares you for, the silence that comes after the sirens fade. The adrenaline drains, the uniforms come off, and what's left is a room full of people who have seen too much and still have to keep going. Training teaches you how to respond to violence, but it doesn't teach you how to carry the weight once the danger has passed. In Uvalde, I watched first responders searching for something they couldn't articulate, something solid to hold onto when answers, control, and certainty were gone.

After watching the work of the Gideons at Uvalde and seeing Steve's work with the Gideon's organization, I decided to join myself. I've handed out Bibles in parking lots, jails, and outside public schools. Every time, someone's fingers tremble when they take one; that's what keeps me coming back. Broken people are searching for answers, and those answers can only be found in one book. If you find yourself looking for answers, and you only want to read one book of the Bible, I suggest you start with John.

I now have access to Bibles and regularly give them out to people. Seeing the reaction of most people when you offer them a free Bible is so impactful. Children's faces light up, adults sometimes have a longing in their eyes. It's not like that with everyone I have offered a Bible to. A few people had flat out said, "No thank you," to the Bible, but in my experience, most people will graciously take the free Bible offered to them.

My wife and I, along with my mother-in-law, took a trip to Boston, Massachusetts, to visit the historical sites in and around the city. While in Boston, at the public transit stop for Harvard University, I saw another Gideon with a box of Bibles handing them out to anyone who wanted one. It's not forcing anyone to take one; it's offering it to them in a public area. No tragic incident had occurred; it was one man doing what he could to offer the hope and grace found within its pages.

I hand it over. Some open it immediately and start reading; some tuck it under their arm and walk away and some refuse it. Either way, my job is done. I am just trying to do my part in fulfilling the Great Commission so no one can say they did not ever hear about God's plan of salvation through Jesus Christ. I can offer them a free book, but what they do with it is between them and God.

CHAPTER FORTY SIX

CONCLUSION

MY CAREER WAS NEVER A STRAIGHT LINE; IT WAS MORE like a heartbeat on a monitor. The spikes of danger, the drops into darkness, a steady strum of routine, all carried by a stubborn refusal to quit. I've chased felons through fields and alleys, held my breath as the bagpipes wailed while standing at attention for the fallen officers. I've walked away from jobs that attempted to grind me into the dust. I've been hit, cut, scorched, doubted, fired, lifted up, and knocked down again.

But the real story isn't just about the violence or the chaos of the badge. It's the pull, stronger than the adrenaline and fear, between me and God.

Every high point in my career lined up with the moments I walked with Him. Every collapse came when I had drifted away, convinced I could do it all on my own. Every single time the world went dark, every time I hit rock bottom, He was still there, standing in the same place, steady and patient, just waiting for me to return home.

I was the one who had wandered. I was the one who chose the shadows. But it was God who pulled me back into the light. Looking back now, it's painfully clear. When I do things my way, things shatter. When I walk with Him, even the hardest paths level out beneath my feet. I've seen humanity at its worst, broken families, dead children, grieving spouses, the kind of cruelty that leaves a stain you feel deep in your bones.

I've also seen redemption that no one could ever explain. Grace in the middle of gunfire. Mercy where none should exist. A life saved in the final second. A heart changed in a jail cell. Hope where it shouldn't grow.

Somehow, through all of it, I kept surviving what should have destroyed me. The nights I almost gave up. The days I thought God had forgotten me. He hadn't. Not once.

Today, I am still serving my community. Still wearing the badge. Still walking into the unknown like I have my entire adult life. But I am not walking alone anymore because I finally understand what happens when I try.

I carry scars, physical and emotional, but they aren't signs of defeat. They're proof. Proof that I was broken, reshaped, rebuilt, and sharpened for a purpose bigger than myself. My story isn't over, and neither is the work God is doing for me. I know this: If I ever forget where I came from, I'll lose where I am going. If I ever walk away from him again, I know exactly what waits for me in the dark.

I choose light. I choose a path that saved me. I choose the God who never once let go.

Because of that, I'm still here. Scarred, steadier, stronger, and finally whole.

A WORD FROM STEPHEN HINTON

SOME BOOKS INFORM. OTHERS INSPIRE. AND THEN there are those rare works that tell the truth so honestly that they confront the reader with the deeper questions of life itself. Scars of the Badge by Tom Lee is one of those books.

At its core, this book is not just about law enforcement, trauma, or the weight carried behind the badge. It is about life... its difficulties and its victories, its failures and its miracles. Tom Lee captures with striking clarity what it means to live in a broken world... saving lives while searching for purpose, healing, and redemption. His story reminds us that success and struggle often walk side by side, and that scars whether physical or emotional tell a story that often repeats itself.

What makes "Scars of the Badge" especially powerful is its unflinching honesty about the inner life of a person. Tom Lee shows that you can achieve professional success, earn respect, and appear strong on the outside, yet still be unraveling on the inside. Life has a way of exposing the truth... that external accomplishments mean very little if one's spiritual condition is neglected. A person can climb to the highest ranks, only to lose everything if their foundation is unstable.

The book makes a compelling case that alignment with the Creator of heaven and earth… Jesus Christ is not optional… it is critical. Your spiritual condition shapes your decisions, your values, and your understanding of right and wrong. Without that divine alignment, even well-intended choices can lead you down destructive paths. With it, clarity begins to replace confusion, and wisdom begins to guide your actions.

Lee's story affirms a timeless truth: God has a plan and a purpose for your life, and that purpose does not end at death. In fact, it begins here and now through a relationship with Jesus Christ. Christianity is not presented as a distant belief system or a moral checklist, but as a living relationship that transforms how you navigate life and where you will spend eternity. When you commit yourself to Christ, everything changes… not because life becomes easy, but because you are no longer walking alone.

Through his journey, Tom Lee demonstrates that surrendering to Christ brings a new way of seeing and deciding. Choices become anchored in biblical truth and principles rather than fear, pride, or impulse. We all strive to make good decisions in relationships, careers, finances… but human wisdom has limits. The Creator knows us better than we know ourselves. HE understands our wounds, our motivations, and our potential, and HE desires to be involved in every aspect of our lives.

Scars of the Badge is ultimately a testimony to the eternal power of that relationship. Lee's transformation reveals that healing does not come from rank, recognition, or perseverance alone, but from surrender. His story is a reminder that trauma is real, redemption can heal, your life can have meaning, and no scar is beyond God's ability to heal and use for good.

This book does more than tell a story… it issues an invitation. An invitation to examine one's own spiritual condition, to consider the consequences of walking through life alone, and to discover what changes when faith becomes your foundation. Tom Lee was given a second chance and discovered that truth firsthand, and through his story, he offers it to the reader who may not be granted a second chance. Receive the free gift of salvation… eternal life through repentance and belief in Christ… Romans 10:9-10.

Stephen Hinton

A FINAL WORD

If this book meant something to you, you're not alone.

These stories were written for the people who have seen too much, carried too much, or felt like no one understands what the weight of the job can do to a person. If you saw yourself in these pages, I hope you know your story matters too.

Leave a Review

One of the most meaningful ways you can support this book is by leaving an honest review on Amazon or wherever you purchased this book.

Reviews help this message reach other first responders and families who may need it. Even a few sentences can make a difference.

Stay Connected

If you'd like to follow future projects, updates, or conversations around first responder wellness, you can connect with me online:

www.scarsofthebadge.com

There you can find updates, resources, and ways to stay in touch.

Share the Message

If you know a first responder, veteran, or family member who might benefit from this book, consider sharing it with them. Sometimes the right book finds someone at the right time.

Thank you for reading Scars of the Badge.

Thank you for caring about the people behind the uniform.

— Tom Lee

ACKNOWLEDGEMENTS

I AM DEEPLY GRATEFUL TO THE MANY PEOPLE WHO helped to bring this book to life. My high school English teacher, Cathey Ondrusek, made it her mission, twenty-five years after I graduated, to read my work and help begin the editorial process. That kind of dedication is something I will never forget.

I also want to thank Chris Evans, Blair Parke, and Paul Higgins for their guidance and editorial support. I never took an English class beyond high school, and while I've written thousands of police reports in my career, writing a book is an entirely different challenge.

I'm grateful as well to the people who encouraged me to write this book. I had thought about it for years, but I didn't truly begin until others told me these stories were worth putting on paper.

A special thanks goes to Stephen Hinton, whose walk with the Lord helped guide me closer to God in my own life. I am thankful to Calvary Baptist Church, where I provided security for years and, in the process, found my way back to the faith. I am also grateful to the members of The Gideons International, Jefferson County Camp, who lead through service, offer encouragement, and faithfully distribute thousands of New Testaments each year.

ABOUT THE AUTHOR

TOM LEE IS A TEXAS LAW ENFORCE-ment officer with a career spanning patrol, investigations, and crisis response. Over the years, he has answered calls involving suicides, child deaths, violent encounters, and the everyday realities most people never see but first responders carry with them long after a shift ends.

His experiences in uniform, including surviving a crossbow attack in the line of duty, shaped not only his career, but his faith, identity, and understanding of resilience. Through those trials, he learned that survival and healing are not the same, and that strength often looks quieter than people expect.

Scars of the Badge is his first book, written to give an honest look at the human cost of the profession and to encourage open conversations about mental health, faith, and support for first responders.

When he's not working or writing, Tom enjoys time with family, cooking, and mentoring others in law enforcement. He remains committed to serving his community and supporting those who wear the badge.

RESOURCES FOR FIRST RESPONDERS AND FAMILIES

The experiences described in this book are real, and for many in public safety, they are familiar. If you or someone you love is struggling, support is available. Reaching out is not weakness, it's a step toward staying in the fight.

In Immediate Crisis

If you are in immediate danger or considering harming yourself, call 911 or your local emergency number.
You can also contact the 988 Suicide & Crisis Lifeline
Dial or text 988 (U.S.)
Available 24/7, confidential, and free.

First Responder

Copline
A confidential peer-support hotline staffed by retired law enforcement officers.
1-800-COPLINE
www.copline.org

Mental Health & Counseling

Substance Abuse and Mental Health Services Administration (SAMHSA)
Treatment locator and mental health resources.
1-800-662-HELP
www.findtreatment.gov

Faith-Based Support

Many find strength through faith communities, chaplains, or pastoral counseling. If faith is part of your life, consider reaching out to a trusted spiritual leader or local church support ministry.